The Random Book of…

CHRISTOPHER

Jason Dickinson

The Random Book of…

CHRISTOPHER

Well, I didn't know that!

All statistics, facts and figures are correct as of March 31st 2009.

Published By:

Stripe Publishing Ltd
First Floor, 3 St. Georges Place, Brighton, BN1 4GA

Email: info@stripepublishing.co.uk
Web: www.stripepublishing.co.uk

First published 2009

10-digit ISBN: 1-907158-02-2
13-digit ISBN: 978-1-907158-02-5

Printed and bound by Gutenberg Press Ltd., Malta.

Editor: Dan Tester
Illustrations: Jonathan Pugh (www.pughcartoons.co.uk)
Typesetting: Andrew Searle
Cover: Andy Heath

In loving memory of my mum, Doreen

INTRODUCTION

Compiling a book solely based on a solitary name seemed
a quite daunting task at first and perhaps before the age of
the internet it would have been almost impossible, other
than after years and years of research.

Thankfully, the world wide web has condensed the planet
and this book can rightly claim to include people named
Christopher from all corners of the globe.

It would have been easy to print pages and pages on such
a famous historical figure as Christopher Columbus, or a
well known actor such as Christopher Reeve or musician
like Coldplay lead singer Chris Martin, but although these
famous individuals have been covered the delight of this
publication is the lesser known individuals, the majority of
whom most readers will have never even heard of.

From the learned scientists and great people in history to
the dumbest and most stupid people on the planet, if they
were called Christopher then they could well be in the
following pages.

Jason Dickinson – March 2009

MEANING OF CHRISTOPHER

The name **Christopher** evolved from the Greek words
for Christ (Christos) and 'to bear, carry' (phero) which were
combined to produce the name of Christophoros. The
name became prevalent with early Christians who wanted
to show they had Christ in their heart.

The English given name of Christopher came into popular
use in the 15th century.

Most popular boys' names:

In the UK

	Christopher	Most Popular	2nd	3rd
1954	9th	David	John	Stephen
1974	6th	Paul	Mark	David
1984	1st	Christopher	James	David
2003	61st	Jack	Joshua	James
2004	68th	Jack	Joshua	James
2005	77th	Jack	Joshua	James
2006	85th	Jack	Thomas	Oliver
2007	90th	Jack	Thomas	Joshua

In the USA

2003	9th	Jacob	Michael	Joshua
2004	10th	Jacob	Michael	Joshua
2005	9th	Jacob	Michael	Joshua
2006	7th	Jacob	Michael	Joshua
2007	6th	Jacob	Michael	Ethan

<u>Variations</u>

Christopher	Greek
Chris	English
Christof	English
Christofer	English
Christofor	French
Christoffer	Scandinavian
Christoforo	Italian
Christoforus	English
Christophe	French
Christophoros	Greek
Christos	Greek
Cristobel	Spanish
Cristobel	Greek
Christofer	German
Christoffer	German
Cristoforo	Italian
Cristovao	Portuguese
Kester	Scottish
Kit	English
Kitt	English
Kris	English
Kriss	English
Krist	Swedish
Kristof	Hungarian
Kristofer	English
Kristoff	Scandinavian
Kristoffer	Scandinavian
Kristofor	English
Kristofr	Greek
Kristopher	Greek

Kristor	Greek
Krystof	Scandinavian
Krystopher	Scandinavian
Krzysztof	Polish
Stoffel	Greek
Topher	American

<hr/>

INCOGNITO CHRISTOPHER

Frank Skinner

Christopher Graham Collins (b. 1957), award-winning comedian and writer, graduated from Birmingham Polytechnic, with an English degree, spending four years working as a lecturer whilst performing stand-up comedy as an extra-curricular activity. He gave up his job to go full-time in 1989.

After being told by actors' union Equity that a member with his name was already on their books (regulations don't allow two people with the same name), he chose the name of a member of his late father's dominoes team.

Best known for his partnership with David Baddiel, which spawned *Fantasy Football League* (1994-2004) and improvisation show *Baddiel and Skinner Unplanned* (2000-2005), the duo wrote and recorded the Euro 96 football anthem, Three Lions.

Skinner inherited his allegiance to West Bromwich Albion FC from his parents. His father, at the time a player for non-league Spennymoor United, met his mother in a local pub after his team had lost 7-1 to Albion in the late 1930s.

The Notorious B. I. G.

Born **Christopher George Latore Wallace** in New York City in May 1972, Biggie Smalls rose to become one of the greatest hip-hop artists of his generation. However, his career was dogged with controversy and he was arrested on several occasions for drugs and weapons misdemeanours whilst becoming involved in a coastal feud that developed between the East and West hip-hop scenes.

He continued to cut a controversial figure and was heavily criticised in 1995 when he failed to attend an anti-violence hip hop summit after the fatal drive-by shooting of rival Tupac Shakur.

In the early hours of March 9th 1997 he was also a victim of a drive-by shooting and was rushed to the local medical centre where he was pronounced dead, aged just 24. The assailant was never caught and in June 1997 his estranged wife, Faith Evans, and his former producer, Puff Daddy, released I'll Be Missing You as a tribute.

The record became a worldwide smash, hitting the number one spot on both sides of the Atlantic.

C. J. Ramone

The bassist with legendary US punk rock band The
Ramones was born **Christopher Joseph Ward** in
Queens, New York in 1965. He replaced original member
Dee Dee Ramone in 1989 and played his first concert in
Leicester in September of the same year.

All the group members used stage names with a common
surname of Ramone (although none of the musicians were
actually related) and he remained in the band under his
particular pseudonym until they disbanded in 1996.

Rat Scabies

Best known as the drummer in seminal UK band The
Damned, **Christopher Miller** used the colourful stage
name of Rat Scabies. He was a co-founder of the group
in 1976 while the band became the first of the new wave
of UK Punk outfits to release a single, New Rose, which
was described by a music critic as a 'deathless anthem of
nuclear-strength romantic angst'.

In 1984 the group appeared on the BBC's cult TV show
The Young Ones although they are perhaps best known for
their 1986 cover of Barry Ryan's Eloise which reached
number three in the UK charts.

Scabies only spent a year with the group after their formation
but returned in 1978, remaining a constant member until a
fall-out led to his permanent departure in 1995.

In 2005 he collaborated with music journalist **Christopher Dawes** to produce the book *Rat Scabies and the Holy Grail*, the story of grail fanatic Scabies' trips to France and Italy on the trail of the legendary Holy Grail. His parents are founder members of the Saunière Society, a collection of like-minded individuals who seek the truth behind the legend, a fascination they passed on to their son.

Limahl

Christopher Hamill (b. 1958) is best known by his stage name of Limahl (being an anagram of his real surname). After being a member of various 1970s punk bands he struck gold when answering an advert placed in UK music magazine *Melody Maker* by the existing members of the group Kajagoogoo.

The fledgling group was looking for a 'front man who could sing and look good' and shortly after he joined, their track Too Shy hit the number one spot. His outrageous hairstyle and outlandish clothes made him instantly recognisable on the 1980s pop scene but his success was short-lived as internal strife beset the band and he was controversially sacked by the group in 1983.

He achieved minor success as a solo artist but by the mid-1980s he was on the dole!

FACEBOOK CHRISTOPHER

Chris Hughes was a co-founder of the hugely popular social networking online site Facebook. He worked as spokesperson for the site for many years and now acts on a consultancy basis. He acted as co-ordinator of online organising for Barack Obama's successful nomination for U.S. President in 2008.

———❖———

INVENTOR CHRISTOPHER

Although Cambridge-born inventor **Sir Christopher Cockerell** filed dozens of patents in his lifetime he is best remembered as the father of the hovercraft. After having studied engineering at Cambridge University he worked for fifteen years at Marconi, producing 36 inventions for the company for which he received the princely sum of £10 for each one.

During the Second World War he worked on radar systems for the armed forces and in 1950 left Marconi to buy a boat building/hire business on the Norfolk Broads. It was at this point that he started his attempts to prove that a vehicle could effectively float on air, which at the early stages involved baked beans tins, a hairdryer and fireworks!

The idea took many years to develop – Cockerell having to sell many personal possessions to fund the research – but by 1955 he had built a working model out of balsa wood and took out his first patent on the invention.

In 1959 he launched a prototype craft which could carry four men at a speed of 28 miles an hour and the first commercial hovercraft crossed the English Channel in 1959. For many years he fought to gain the financial reward for his invention and passed away on June 1st 1999 – appropriately on the 40th anniversary of the launch of the hovercraft – at the grand old age of 88.

British inventor **Chris Elvey** hit the headlines in 2007 when he succeeded in powering a vehicle on chocolate, which duly drove the 4,500 miles to Timbuktu in Mali, Africa!

He created the fuel from 5,000 tonnes of waste chocolate with recycled cooking oil and sugar.

The fuel cost just 15p a litre to produce and he claimed that would take his vehicle 50 miles. The expedition hit some problems on the way – when the drivers hit the Pyrenees – as the additive-free fuel started freezing and after a wait of two days they had no choice but to add some standard fossil fuel!

However, the vehicle crossed the Sahara desert and made it all the way to Mali proving that bio-fuel is a credible alternative as the world's fossil fuel reserves start to run dry.

Popular UK television show *Dragons' Den* usually sends most inventors home with a flea in their ear but in 2006 **Chris Haines** was different as Theo Paphitis and Deborah Meaden backed his invention of the Safe T Light.

The light does not fail in a power cut and a part can be detached and used as a torch, ending the days of sifting through drawers in the dark for that torch or box of matches. His invention won Chris the British Invention 2006 Gold Award. He also won a Gold Medal from the BIS (British Inventors Society).

When **Christopher Monckton** invented the puzzle *Eternity* he was so confident that it would not be cracked quickly he offered a £1m reward to the first person to do so, after the game was launched in 1999.

The former policy advisor to Margaret Thatcher was however in for a shock as after just over a year – two years less than Monckton had expected – an unemployed mathematician, Alex Selby, cracked it!

He had received *Eternity* as a Christmas present and it was not until the following November that he attempted to solve the game, which features 209 jigsaw pieces, all of the same colour, between seven and eleven sides each.

He shared his winnings with former colleague Oliver Riordan – one of the world's top mathematicians – who helped him solve the puzzle, helped also by a computer program the duo wrote.

The inventor had hoped to pay the prize money on revenues generated by the sale – plus an insurance policy for the remainder – but was delighted the puzzle had been solved although he did have to sell his £1.5m stately home in Scotland to pay the reward!

Wisconsin newspaperman **Christopher Latham Sholes**
(1819-1890) is credited as the inventor of the modern-day
typewriter. His first version was patented in 1868 when
Sholes, in conjunction with Samuel Soule, invented a
numbering machine before his friend, Carlos Glidden,
joined after suggesting the pair should try to make a
machine that printed letters.

The first patent was prone to breaking down and it needed
investor James Densmore to give the final financial push
the invention needed when he bought out both Soule and
Glidden.

The final product was patented in 1871. Remington
purchased the patent outright with Sholes receiving
$12,000. Densmore used his investor nous by choosing to
take a royalty on sales, eventually earning $1.5m!

Although the typewriter has been largely superseded by the PC
one legacy of Sholes is the QWERTY keyboard, named after
the position of the first six letters at the top left hand side.

This was more accident than design as his first attempts
at using the keyboard resulted in the collision of many of
the bars holding the letters. He decided to split the most
commonly used letters on either side of the keyboard to
avoid such situations, hence the layout of the modern-day
keyboard was born.

ICE AGE CHRISTOPHER

When fell walker **Christopher Dagleish** failed to return
to his Lake District hotel in November 2007 a search party
was dispatched but returned having failed to locate the
missing man.

However, over a month later the office worker from Harrow,
Middlesex was discovered near Broughton-in-Furniss, entombed
in a two-inch thick block of ice, still wearing his spectacles.

———◆———

ICE DANCING CHRISTOPHER

Known as 'Bowman the Showman' at the height of his fame
in the 1980s, twice US Ice Dancing Champion **Christopher
Bowman** had first shot to fame as a child actor – appearing in
U.S. television series *Little House on the Prairie*.

In the late 1980s he won silver, and then bronze, at the
World Ice Dancing Championships and it was common
for girls to scream and throw flowers at Bowman after a
performance.

He finished fourth in the 1992 Winter Olympic Games –
despite having landed a highly difficult 'triple axel' – and
after just missing out on a medal he toured for a year
with his own troupe, The Ice Capades. Sadly those glory
days proved relatively fleeting and after years of drug and
alcohol abuse he was found dead, aged just 40, in a Los
Angeles Motel room in January 2008.

The Random Book of...

His weight had ballooned to over 300lbs and the autopsy
was unable to determine whether he died of a drug
overdose or natural causes.

Nottingham-born **Christopher Colin Dean OBE** (b.
1958) is best known for his ice dancing partnership with
Jayne Torvill that wooed audiences all over the world.
Their free dance to the music of Ravel's *Boléro* at the 1984
Sarajevo Winter Olympics received the maximum mark
of nine 6.0 scores – the only time this has ever occurred.
The performance was watched by an incredible UK TV
audience of 24 million.

The duo turned professional directly after the games
and ten years later they returned to the Olympic arena
after authorities relaxed their rules regarding professional
skaters and won a bronze at the 1994 Lillehammer
games.

Dean is married to his second wife, U.S. skater Jill Trenary,
and resides in Colorado Springs, Colorado.

BASEBALL CHRISTOPHER

When 11-year-old **Chris Scala** chose baseball legend Babe
Ruth as the subject for a school dress up project in 1996
little did he realise that he would set off a chain of events
what would greatly enrich his family.

When his great-grandmother – Viola Bevilaque – heard about his task she found something in her attic to go with the outfit – a long forgotten ball signed by the 1920s baseball star.

The baseball had been gathering dust in a box, along with other possessions of her late husband, who had been gifted the ball back in 1927. An inscription inside the box provided the requisite provenance that the ball was in fact the first one ever hit by Ruth for a home run in the famous Yankee Stadium in New York.

At auction in 1998 the ball sold for $126,500!

CAUGHT RED-HANDED CHRISTOPHER

When **Christopher Guther** robbed the London Cheapside branch of The Royal Bank of Scotland in 2003 he got away with more than just £4,200 in cash. Unbeknown to the bungling robber he also carried off several anti-theft dye cartridges, disguised as bundles of notes, which duly exploded minutes later to cover Christopher head to toe in red dye!

He ran from the scene but was followed by a taxi driver who tailed him to a 20p automatic toilet before calling the police.

He'd sought refuge in the public convenience but was soon surrounded by cops and in true Hollywood style an officer called through a loud hailer; "Come out with your hands up!"

He threw out his fake gun and after a siege lasting a whole three minutes he was taken into custody, being sentenced to ten years in jail when his case went to court.

⟫◆⟪

TALL CHRISTOPHER

An international basketball player for the Great Britain team in the late 1960s and early 1970s, **Christopher Greener** was, for over 40 years, the tallest man in the United Kingdom. Born in November 1943, from a very young age Greener had a tumour at the base of his pituitary gland – an organ that controls the release of human growth hormone.

The tumour caused his pituitary gland to grow several times larger than that of an average person and by 1970 he had grown to a height of 7ft 6½ins. (2.3 metres). In fact, if surgeons had not operated to remove the tumour when Christopher was 27 he would have still continued to grow indefinitely.

It was not until 1970 that he had finally been correctly diagnosed with the condition known as pituitary gigantism – a common factor in many larger-than-life human beings.

As well as being an obvious choice for the aforementioned sport of basketball, he also worked as an actor – filling many height-based comic roles – and is perhaps best known for playing the Circus Giant in David Lynch's *The Elephant Man*.

He was also a regular face on television and appeared in the U.S. TV special *The World's Tallest People* and in 2002 was a special guest on Vic Reeves and Bob Mortimer's *Shooting Stars*.

<hr/>

CHRISTOPHER QUOTES

"Working with her is like being hit over the head with a Valentine's Day card"
Actor **Christopher Plummer** on working with Julie Andrews

"Was this the face that launched a thousand ships, and burnt the topless towers of Ileum?"
Playwright/Author **Christopher Marlowe**

"So many of our dreams at first seem impossible, then they seem improbable, and then, when we summon the will, they become inevitable"
Christopher Reeve at the Democratic Convention in August 1996

"Riches don't make a rich man, they only make him busier"
Explorer **Christopher Columbus**

"You know the world is going crazy when the best rapper is a white guy, the best golfer is a black guy, the tallest guy in the NBA is Chinese, the Swiss hold the America's Cup, France is accusing the US of

arrogance, Germany doesn't want to go to war, and the three most powerful men in America are named 'Bush', 'Dick' and 'Colon'. Need I say more?"
Chris Rock

"I've got five stepmothers. My dad's been approved for a Marriage Licence Gold Card 'I now pronounce you man and wife' (sound of a credit card imprinter) 'Sign here, bottom copy's yours'"
Chris Titus

"Asking a working writer what he thinks about critics is like asking a lamp-post what it feels about dogs"
Writer **Christopher Hampton**

"If she tries to blackmail me, I'll throw her out a higher window"
Max Schreck (played by **Christopher Walken**) in *Batman Returns*

"Black people dominate sports in the United States; 20% of the population and 90% of the final four. We own this shit. Basketball, baseball, football, golf, tennis, and as soon as they make a heated hockey rink, we'll take that shit too"
Chris Rock (again)

"Procrastination is like having a credit card; it is lots of fun until you get the bill"
Author **Christopher Parker**

"I am Connor MacLeod. I was born in 1518 in the village of Glenfinnan on the shores of Loch Shiel. And I am immortal"
Christopher Lambert in *Highlander*

"The most interesting persons are always those who have nothing special to do: children, nurses, policemen and actors at 11 o'clock in the morning"
Writer **Christopher Morley** in *Travels in Philadelphia*

"I don't need to be made to look evil. I can do that on my own"
Christopher Walken (again)

"High heels were invented by a woman who had been kissed on the forehead"
Christopher Morley

"Nothing succeeds like the appearance of success"
Christopher Lasch

"Anything a woman asks for is really a demand"
Christopher Curtis

RECORD-BREAKING CHRISTOPHER

North American self-styled 'Jim Carey of Magic',
Christopher Linn holds the world record of 'making a
balloon dog with both hands behind the back' at just 5.94
seconds.

He smashed the previous record by a whole second and if
you were just a little bit curious he tied a poodle and not a
sausage dog!

If that wasn't enough he is also the proud owner of the
record for card throwing when he managed to throw
114 playing cards a distance of at least 12 feet in one
minute...

In May 2005 **Chris Camp** of Illinois, USA set a new
world record when he cracked a bullwhip an astonishing
222 times in only 60 seconds, beating the previous record of
214 set by a Minneapolis cowboy in 2004.

Scotland's rugby union international **Chris Paterson**
(b. 1978) became his country's record points scorer. The
June 2008 defeat in Argentina – 21-15 – meant he overtook
the long standing record of 667 set by Gavin Hastings. A
few days later, against the same opposition, in Buenos Aires,
he became Scotland's most capped player, winning cap
number 88, again surpassing Hastings.

Independent candidate **Christopher John Talbot**
was one of 26 people who fought the Haltemprice and
Howden by-election on July 11th 2008. As well as boasting
the highest numbers of candidates in UK electoral
history, a record number – 23 – lost their £500 deposits
while the Green Party secured their best ever finish in a
Parliamentary election, finishing second.

Neither Labour, the Liberal Democrats, UKIP, nor the BNP
fielded candidates for a seat won by Tory David Davis with
17,113 votes. Other budding MPs included:

Mad Cow-Girl	412 votes
(The Official Monster Raving Loony Party)	
Gemma Garrett	521 votes
(Miss Great Britain Party)	
David Bishop	44 votes
(Church of the Militant Elvis Party)	

Former Eurovision song contest singer Ronnie Carroll
(Make Politicians History Party) failed in his attempt to poll
no votes whatsoever after receiving an almost respectable
29! Biggest problem for the officials was fitting all the names
on a ballot paper...

⟫⟩◆⟨⟪

EXPLORER CHRISTOPHER

Arguably the most famous Christopher of all, Italian-
born navigator, adventurer and coloniser **Christopher
Columbus** made four voyages to the Americas:

1492   Landed in the Bahamas, Cuba and Haiti. His
        crew brought back some natives but unfortunately
        modern evidence suggests they also brought back
        a rather more unwelcome guest, syphilis, which
        would kill around five million people.

1493   Explored and named several islands including
        Montserrat, St. Kitts and The Virgin Islands while also
        landing at Puerto Rico and the Dominican Republic.

1498   Landed in Trinidad and explored the northern tip
        of South America, while discovering, and naming,
        Grenada and Tobago.

1502   'Discovered' many Central American countries,
        including Honduras, Nicaragua, Panama and
        Costa Rica. After being stranded on the island
        of Jamaica, his great knowledge of the stars
        ensured his men were well fed and looked after
        by the natives after Columbus correctly predicted
        a lunar eclipse, greatly impressing and somewhat
        intimidating the locals!

Soon after his death in 1506 the continent of the Americas
was named. His legacy is immeasurable with the United
States considering him the founder of the New World. A
multitude of cities, towns and streets have been named after
Columbus all over the Americas.

SPOOKY CHRISTOPHER

In December 2002 two motorists reported to local police that they had seen a car lose control and swerve off the A3 road at Burpham, Surrey. The officers carried out an extensive search of the area and eventually discovered a car in thick undergrowth with a long-dead driver at the wheel.

However, the occupant, **Christopher Chandler**, had been reported missing by his brother five months earlier…

⟫◆⟪

THOMAS THE TANK CHRISTOPHER

Ringo Starr is known for two roles – the drummer with legendary band The Beatles and of course as the voice of Thomas the Tank Engine in the much-loved animated children's cartoons.

The first 26 books in the 'Thomas' Railway series were written by the Rev. W. Awdry – adapted from a story he told to his sick son, Christopher, back in 1942. In 1983 **Christopher Awdry** took over from his father as the author of the Thomas books, starting with *Really Useful Engines*, and has since published:

Toby, Trucks and Trouble (1988)
Thomas and Fat Controller's Engines (1995)
Thomas and Victoria (2007)

In addition to the Thomas volumes written so far by Christopher Awdry, he has also penned various other 'Thomas' books including two concentrating on railway safety, which went to every primary school and library in the UK. These were subsequently turned into colouring books by Virgin Trains to teach small children about the dangers of railways.

———◆———

RULING CHRISTOPHER

Prince Christopher was born in Imperial Russia in 1888, to George I of Greece and Olga, former Queen of Russia. He was known as 'Christo' to his family and like all of his siblings Christopher was a polyglot, meaning he could read, write, speak and understand languages other than his native tongue. He was fluent in Greek, English, Danish, Russian, French and German.

Rather bizarrely he used Greek to converse with his siblings, spoke to his parents in English while they spoke to one another in German!

He declined the thrones of Portugal, Lithuania and Albania as he did not want the stresses that power brought and courted controversy in 1920 when he married an American divorcee – they were engaged for six years as legal teams battled to sort out his impending marriage to a mere commoner!

His new wife's wealth – inherited from her deceased millionaire husband – greatly helped the Greek Royal

Family during their 1920s exile. A direct descendant was one Philip of Greece, better known in the UK as HRH Prince Philip.

Christopher I ruled Denmark between 1252 and 1259. His short tenure was turbulent, having to cope with two peasant revolts, the second because of a property tax, while he ran into major problems with the most powerful of Denmark's Archbishops.

The Holy man refused to recognise his son, Eric, as the future King of Denmark so Christopher humiliated him by forcing him to wear the clothes of a fool and cast him into prison.

It was that act that would prove Christopher's downfall as he died suddenly after taking 'Holy Communion' in May 1259. He is believed to have drunk poisoned wine taken from the hands of an Abbot who was seeking revenge for the mistreatment of the Archbishop.

Christopher II was the grandson of Christopher I and ruled Denmark on two separate occasions; 1320-1326 and 1329-1332. History has not exactly been kind to the second Christopher monarch as the history books paint him as a weak, unreliable and incapable tyrant!

He is known as the King 'who mortgaged Denmark to the Germans' although his predecessors had started the common practice of mortgaging large parts of their estate to raise money!

Christopher III was King of the Danes between 1439 and 1448 and also ruled Sweden (1441-48) and Norway (1442-48). His reign was also dogged by peasant revolts with a 25,000-strong Jutland revolt posing a serious threat to his power.

However, before he could raise an army the Noblemen of Jutland raised their own force but were over-confident and were massacred by the peasant army; the leader was killed, dismembered and his parts sent to different towns in the area to act as a warning!

An army led by Christopher eventually suppressed the revolt with any peasants that survived forced to work as slaves. It was Christopher who made Copenhagen the capital of Denmark (1443).

The modern German south-west state of Baden-Württemberg was once an autonomous region called simply Württemberg and was ruled between 1550 and 1568 by **Duke Christoph.**

He fathered twelve children with his wife, Anna Maria, and was responsible for renovating the famous castle in the capital city of the region, Stuttgart, which still stands today.

The most famous individual born in the region was undoubtedly brilliant scientist Albert Einstein while there is a museum in the New Castle (built in the 18th century) to former resident of the city, Claus Schenk Graf von Stauffenberg, who tried to assassinate Nazi leader Adolf Hitler in July 1944.

Christopher Bathory (1530-1581) was the Prince of Transylvania in the 16th century.

⟫◈⟪

STUPID CHRISTOPHER

When **Christopher Johns** went on trial for drug possession in Pontiac, Michigan in March 1999 he stated that he had been searched without a warrant. The court prosecutor said the arresting officer did not need a warrant as a 'bulge' in the defendant's jacket suggested he may have been carrying a firearm.

Christopher, who happened to be wearing the same jacket in court that day, strongly denied this was the case and promptly handed it over to the residing judge so he could see for himself. The judge discovered a packet of cocaine in the pocket and laughed so much that he required a five-minute recess to compose himself...

When Arizona police responded to a call about a woman trying to cash a forged cheque they gave chase when she drove off with an accomplice. The twosome went through several red lights with the police hot on their tail before breaking down in the middle of the desert and fleeing into the wilderness.

They quickly became entangled in a cholla cactus and as hospital workers plucked cactus spines from his body, a tearful **Christopher Psomas** admitted, "I am so stupid".

PARANOID CHRISTOPHER

The March 2005 death of 19-year-old Michigan resident **Christopher** was described by law enforcement officers as 'unusual' and 'complicated'. The teenager had spent the evening drinking large volumes of alcohol in his front room but when he ran dry he came to the conclusion that his neighbour must have stolen his booze!

Knife in hand, he went next door to confront his neighbour. However, when there was no response at his door, Christopher returned to his apartment to plan his revenge on the light fingered bottle thief, eventually deciding that the perfect revenge would be to stab himself and blame the neighbour!

A witness saw him enter the bathroom and call 911 to report that his neighbour had committed the crime and come back out with blood pouring from his chest.

Unfortunately, he was so good at inflicting the wounds that he bled to death before officers could even reach the scene. It later transpired that he had stabbed himself once and decided it did not look bad enough but the second attempt hit the spot as the knife plunged straight into his heart, giving him all of two minutes to live.

The irony of the whole sorry tale was that his neighbour was not home…

WHAT DOES CHRISTOPHER ACTUALLY MEAN, EXACTLY?
A kid who is always up to party and have a good time.

USAGE:
"Dude, I don't want go to that party unless Chris comes."

⬥

WHAT DOES CHRISTOPHER ACTUALLY MEAN, EXACTLY?
A Christopher (or a Chris) is someone who wears red
cardigans, goes to shows, and aims their legs in 90 degree
angles. They also sport a curly haircut and are generally
taller than 90% of the population.

USAGE:
"Is Chris going to the show?"
"Obviously."

⬥

WHAT DOES CHRISTOPHER ACTUALLY MEAN, EXACTLY?
A crazy chap that went to your Secondary School.

USAGE:
*"Chris was the craziest kid I remember. One time he got a referral for
splashing in a puddle. Or the other time he got suspended for dipping a
tampon in red soda!"*

WHAT DOES CHRISTOPHER ACTUALLY MEAN, EXACTLY?
Steals their friends' drinks.

USAGE:
"Who stole my drink, who pulled a Chris?"

⬖

WHAT DOES CHRISTOPHER ACTUALLY MEAN, EXACTLY?
Gets really drunk but will not admit it.

USAGE:
"Are you chrissed?"
"No, I'm totally sober"

⬖

WHAT DOES CHRISTOPHER ACTUALLY MEAN, EXACTLY?
From the Greek word 'Christof', meaning awesome, totally
dominating and a sex god! Often used in reference to
someone from school you'll always remember.

USAGE:
Boy: *"Do you still remember Chris?"*
Girl: *"Was he that awesome, totally dominating sex god? Yeah, I
think I do, what a Chris."*

What does Christopher actually mean, exactly?
Someone who has the tendency to forget where they placed the most practical and mundane belongings.

USAGE:
"Mate, Chris left his wallet at my house again."
"That is such a Chris thing to do."

Generous Christopher

In 2003 city financier **Chris Hohn** (b. 1967) set up The Children's Investment Fund (TCI) so he could give a percentage of the earnings directly to its charitable sister organisation – the Children's Investment Fund Foundation (CIFF).

The foundation, run by his wife Jamie, has given monies to the likes of the Clinton Federation for the treatment of HIV and AIDS, an orphan project in Malawi and to an emergency aid project in Darfur.

However, in June 2008 Chris Hohn made the headlines when he gifted his wife's charity a staggering £466 million – almost half a billion pounds – which is the largest ever charity donation made by a British citizen.

The London couple are now Britain's most generous philanthropists after having donated over £800 million to worthwhile causes in just four years.

TRAFFIC OFFICER CHRISTOPHER

PC Christopher Rowley hit the headlines in June 2004 when it was revealed he was working for the Hertfordshire police as a traffic officer despite the small but relatively important fact that he could not drive!

The 26-year-old officer had failed his driving test twice and was being ferried around by fellow officers as they policed the M1, A1 and M25. Incredibly, he had been assigned to the traffic cops despite his lack of a driving licence which meant he could not even perform such simple tasks as moving a vehicle at the scene of an accident or stopping offenders for speeding.

———

CHRISTOPHER PLACES

Christopher	Franklin County, Illinois, USA
Christopher	Chattahoochee County, Georgia, USA
Christopher	King County, Washington State, USA
Christopher	Newton County, Missouri, USA
Christopher	Perry County, Kentucky, USA
Christopher Lake	Saskatchewan, Canada
Christopher Lake	Western Australia
Christopher	New Brunswick, Canada
Christopher River	New Zealand
Christopher Acre	Rochdale
Christopher	Cardiff, Wales
Christopher Street	Manhattan, New York, USA
Christopher Close	Louth

Christopher Court	Northampton
Christopher Crescent	Poole
Christopher Road	Wolverhampton
Christopher Creek	Arizona, USA
Christopher Nagar	Tamil Nadu, India
Christopher S. Bond Bridge	Hermann, Missouri
Christopher S. Bond Bridge	Kansas City, Missouri
Christopher Street Pier	Manhattan, New York

CHRISTOPHER AWARDS

The Christophers were founded in 1945 by American, Father James Kelly with the motto:

'It's better to light one candle than to curse the darkness: Affirming the highest values of the human heart.'

From the late 1940s the award was given to individuals in the entertainment and communications industry and has many categories, including **Christopher** Leadership and **Christopher** Life Achievement.

The **Christopher Brennan Award** is an Australian prize given for lifetime achievement in poetry. The award, presented by the Fellowship of Australian Writers, was established in the mid-1970s and named after Antipodean poet Christopher Brennan (1870-1932).

The **Christopher Ewart-Biggs Memorial Prize** has been awarded annually since 1977 with a stated goal of:

Promoting peace and reconciliation in Ireland, a greater understanding between the peoples of Britain and Ireland or closer co-operation between partners of the European Community.

The award was named after a British ambassador to Eire who was killed by the IRA in 1976.

<hr>

ELIZABETHAN CHRISTOPHER

Northampton-born **Sir Christopher Hatton** was a powerful figure during the 16th century in England, eventually being appointed Lord Chancellor in 1587 after having first been elected to Parliament in 1571.

He cut a dashing figure at court and took the eye of Queen Elizabeth – she had appointed him captain of her bodyguard in 1572 – and it was not only Mary Queen of Scots (Mary Stuart) that alleged the couple were more than mere confidantes.

He was knighted in 1578, effectively becoming the Queen's voice in Parliament such was his power, while the Monarch frequently showed her affection for Hatton by bestowing extravagant and outlandish gifts upon him. It was Hatton who ordered the warrant for Mary Stuart's execution in 1587. He died a very wealthy man, in November 1591, leaving his estate to his nephew after never marrying.

TWINKIE CHRISTOPHER

North American favourite the 'Twinkie' – a sponge cake
bar filled with cream – was first introduced into the US
market back in 1930. However, it needed British-born
Christopher Sell to give the staple favourite a new twist
in 2000 when he decided to deep fry the Twinkie at his New
York-based Park Slope Chip Shop.

The idea of deep frying items such as Mars Bars first
originated in Scotland, later spreading to northern England,
and Sell was already offering such items on his menu at his
English style eatery when, almost as a joke, he tossed one
into his fat fryer to see what occurred.

The final article proved quite tasty and a favourable review
from a *New York Times* food writer meant the rest is history.
The treat, with a waist-expanding 400 calories and 28
grams of fat, was even served by one Seattle Fair vendor
with sugar and chocolate sauce on top. He sold 26,000 in 18
days at one event…

WINNIE THE POOH CHRISTOPHER

The stories created by author Alan Alexander Milne
surrounding the exploits of Pooh, Tigger, Piglet and Eeyore
have arguably become the best loved children's books of
all-time.

It was the childhood of the author's son, **Christopher Robin Milne** (1920-1996) that proved the initial inspiration for the much-loved characters with Winnie-the-Pooh evolving from a teddy bear that Christopher received on his first birthday, and a real life bear named 'Winnie' who resided at London Zoo.

The child character in the stories was of course based solely on his son who was given the name Christopher Robin when his parents decided to choose a name each to help distinguish their new arrival from other members of the Milne family.

⟾◈⟻

CHRISTOPHER SLANG

In the US State of Vermont the locals use the name of **Christopher** as negative slang for a flatlander (a person who is not born in Vermont or is a visitor) and would be used in a phrase such as "he was from Los Angeles and was a total Christopher".

⟾◈⟻

SAINT CHRISTOPHER

Medieval Christian legend says **St. Christopher** was a giant fearsome man who after first deciding to serve the devil was converted to Christianity by a hermit. He lived in a house by the river and in order to serve Christ he would carry travellers across the water.

One day he carried a small boy across but was inexplicably weighed down – the boy then told Christopher that he was Jesus Christ and that Christopher had carried the weight of the whole world and 'him that created and made all the world upon thy shoulders'.

Mythology says he was martyred in Lycia (modern day Turkey) in the 1st century AD and his story was augmented and re-told as the 'Golden Legend' in the 14th century, leading to his image being artistically portrayed Europe wide – assuring his place amongst the 'Fourteen Holy Helpers'.

He is mainly referred to in modern times as the patron saint of travellers; the cross of St. Christopher being a common sight.

WILDERNESS CHRISTOPHER

When American wanderer **Christopher McCandless** hiked into the Alaskan wilderness in April 1992 it was with the intention of leading a life of solitude.

However, less than five months after waving goodbye to civilisation he died of starvation – aged just 24 – his body weighing just 67 pounds when he was discovered in an abandoned bus he called home. In 1996 Jon Krakauer wrote a book about his life – helped by the diaries McCandless kept – and this was turned into a Sean Penn film of the same name, *Into the Wild*, in 2007.

CAUGHT UP A TREE CHRISTOPHER

Somewhat bizarrely, in April 2004, teenager **Christopher Montero** was caught naked up a tree in New York's Central Park having sex with his transsexual lover!

When the police arrived on the scene the duo started throwing tree branches down on the cops and both were duly arrested. Christopher was sentenced to community work for endangering the officers.

CHRISTOPHER ISLAND

Situated in the Leeward Islands in the West Indies is the two-island nation of St. Kitts & Nevis. The larger island of Saint Kitts was called Liamuiga (fertile land) by the Kalinago Indians who were the last native tribe to settle the island, before the arrival of the Europeans, 5,000 years after it was first inhabited.

It was Christopher Columbus who was the first European to chart the island and for many years it was thought he named the island San Cristobel, after the patron saint.

It has since been discovered that due to a mapping error the island was actually named Saint Jago (Saint James), with the island of Saba – 20 miles away – the real recipient of the St. Christopher moniker.

However, the name stuck and when the British made the island their first colony in the West Indies in 1624 they retained its English form – **St. Christopher's Island**. In the 17th century the name of Christopher was often shortened to Kitt so the paradise soon became Saint Kitt's Island and finally Saint Kitts.

The island remained a colony until 1983 and is now an independent state of the Commonwealth. In September 1998 Hurricane George caused close to $445 million in damage.

CHRISTOPHER SONGS

A handful of songs with Christopher in their title relate to the patron saint with US band Styx's **Christopher, Mr. Christopher** being a lament to the saint's perceived downgrading by the Roman Catholic Church in 1969.

On Tom Waits' 1987 album Frank's Wild Years he implores the saint to watch over him in **Hang On St. Christopher** as he pushed his hot rod car and motorcycle to their limits.

The song was also later covered by Rod Stewart on his 1995 album A Spanner In The Works. Waits also laments the loss of his St. Christopher in Tom Traubert's Blues while the saint is also mentioned in Bon Jovi's 2002 released album Bounce in Right Side Of Wrong.

A St. Christopher song was also penned by former Culture Club singer Boy George on his 2002 debut solo album U Can Never Be 2 Straight.

On his 1986 soundtrack to the motion picture *Under the Cherry Moon*, Prince penned **Christopher Tracey's Parade** while on their 2002 debut album Blackened Sky Scottish rock act Biffy Clyro recorded the song Christopher's River.

Considered by many to be one of the finest singer-songwriters that France has ever produced, Veronique Sanson – best known in the UK for her song Amoureuse, which was a big hit for Kiki Dee in 1973 – wrote the song **Christopher** for her new infant son. It appeared on the 1974 album Le Maudit.

The Love You Save by the Jackson Five, later covered by teen band Hanson, also name checks **Christopher**.

⟹◆⟸

CHRISTOPHER STREET

Although originally called Skinner Road, **Christopher Street** – renamed in 1799 when the land was acquired by Charles Christopher Amos – in the New York City borough of Manhattan rose to worldwide prominence in the late 1970s as the centre of the gay rights movement.

Back in the 19th century the street was split in half between the working class western end and the bohemian eastern end while race riots erupted in 1932 between striking white longshoremen and black strike breakers.

As recently as the 1920s and 1930s several bars on the street catered to gay men but it was not until a police raid on the Stonewall Inn on June 27th 1969 that the movement came to international prominence. The riot that ensued is widely recognised as the start of the gay liberation movement.

Famous people to have lived on Christopher Street include Yoko Ono while purely by coincidence a street that intersects Christopher Street is called Gay Street!

⟫⊷⟪

MIDDLE-EARTH CHRISTOPHER

Highly acclaimed writer J. R. R. Tolkien published classics – *The Hobbit* and *The Lord of the Rings* trilogy – but appointed his youngest son, **Christopher**, as literary executor before his death. As a child Christopher had delighted at tales of Bilbo Baggins and as a teenager helped draw the maps included in the books.

He undertook the arduous task of trying to bring together all his father's unpublished works, which in many cases involved hand written notes which had been revised several times over – many from fifty years prior.

However, in conjunction with fantasy author Guy Gavriel Kay, he edited J. R. R. Tolkein's *The Silmarillion* in 1977, *Unfinished Tales* in 1980 and a series of twelve volumes entitled *The History of Middle-earth* between 1983 and 1986.

As recently as April 2007 Christopher published *The Children of Hurin*, which his father had started back in 1918 but had abandoned in the late 1950s after several re-writes. The 'new' book sold over a million copies in its first few weeks of release.

FOOTBALLING CHRISTOPHER

When **Chris Coward** played for Stockport County against Sheffield Wednesday in 2005 at the age of just 16 years and 30 days he became the youngest ever player to appear in the Football League Cup competition.

During the 1986-87 season Glasgow Rangers goalkeeper **Chris Woods** did not concede a goal for 1,196 minutes, setting a new record in British soccer.

Christofer Heimeroth is a German-born goalkeeper who plays for Borussia Mőnchengladbach in his home country.

While playing for Tow Law Town, **Chris Waddle** (b. 1960) worked for a company that made spices for sausages and pies. He became the most expensive British footballer when he transferred from Tottenham Hotspur to Olympic Marseille for £4.25m in July 1989. During his time at Spurs he collaborated with Glen Hoddle on the top 20 hit Diamond Lights.

He suffered the heartbreak of missing the decisive penalty in England's World Cup semi-final shoot out with Germany in 1990 but was a huge success in France where he was nicknamed 'Magic Chris' by fans.

He returned to England and was voted Football Writers' Player of the Year at Sheffield Wednesday in 1993. He continued to play into his early 40s and is now a regular voice on Radio Five Live.

French international **Christophe Dugarry** (b. 1972) enjoyed an outstanding career for both club and country. He played in both the 1998 World Cup Final – France beat Brazil 3-0 – and the European Championship Final two years later where his country beat Italy 2-1.

In total he played 55 times for France while at club level he represented the likes of Marseille, AC Milan and Barcelona, ending his career in England with Birmingham City in 2005.

Chris Kamara (b. 1957) enjoyed a long career appearing in over 700 league games and went on to manage both Bradford City and Stoke City. He is now a well known face on Sky Sports' *Goals on Sunday* and his live links to the studio during the Saturday afternoon football programme have become almost legendary; his overexcited cry "Unbelievable, Jeff!" to host Jeff Stelling becoming his trademark catchphrase.

Known only by the name Christopher, French-born **Christopher de Almeida** is the goalkeeper for Portuguese club C. S. Maritimo. Although not Portuguese by birth he has represented the country at under-21 level and is seen as the eventual successor to national keeper Vítor Baía.

A selection of Christophers playing in the English leagues during the 2007-08 season:

Blackburn Rovers	**Chris Samba**
Bristol Rovers	**Chris Carruthers** and **Chris Lines**
Burnley	**Chris McCann**
~~Cardiff City~~	**Chris Gunter**
Carlisle United	**Chris Lumsdon**
Chester City	**Chris Holroyd**
Colchester United	**Chris Coyne**
Coventry City	**Chris Birchall**
Crewe Alexandra	**Chris Flynn** and **Chris McCready**
Dagenham & Redbridge	**Chris Moore**
Darlington	**Chris Palmer**
Fulham	**Chris Baird**
Gillingham/Crewe Alexandra	**Chris Dickson**
Hereford United	**Kris Taylor and Chris Weale**
Huddersfield Town	**Chris Brandon**
Ipswich Town	**Chris Casement**
Luton Town	**Chris Coyne** and **Chris Perry**
Manchester United	**Chris Eagles**
Mansfield Town	**Chris Wood**
Middlesbrough	**Chris Riggott**
Millwall	**Chris Day** and **Chris Hackett**
Northampton Town	**Chris Doig** and **Chris Dunn**
Norwich City	**Chris Brown** and **Chris Martin**
Oldham Athletic	**Chris Taylor**
Plymouth Argyle	**Chris Clark**
Port Vale	**Chris Slater** and **Chris Martin**
Port Vale/Wycombe Wanderers	**Chris Herd**
Queens Park Rangers	**Chris Barker**
Rochdale	**Chris Basham** and **Chris Dagnall**

Rotherham United	**Chris O'Grady**
Stockport County	**Chris Adamson**
Stoke City	**Chris Riggott**
Swansea City	**Kris O'Leary**
Tottenham Hotspur	**Chris Gunter**
Tranmere Rovers	**Chris Greenacre** and **Chris Shuker**
Wigan Athletic	**Chris Kirkland**
Wrexham	**Chris Llewellyn**
Wycombe Wanderers	**Chris Palmer**

OLYMPICS CHRISTOPHER

Winners of Olympic medals 1896-2008

GOLD:

Christopher McKivatt
| Rugby | London | 1908 | Australia |

Christopher Jones
| Polo | Antwerp | 1920 | Great Britain |

Christopher Brasher
| Steeplechase | Melbourne | 1956 | Great Britain |

Christoph Höhne
| 50km Walk | Mexico | 1968 | West Germany |

Christopher Finnegan
| Boxing | Mexico | 1968 | Great Britain |

Christopher Cavanaugh
| Swimming | Los Angeles | 1984 | USA |

Christopher Jacobs
| Swimming | Seoul | 1988 | USA |

Christopher Mullin
| Basketball | Barcelona | 1992 | USA |

Chris Boardman
| Cycling | Barcelona | 1992 | Great Britain |

Christopher Reitz
| Hockey | Barcelona | 1992 | Germany |

Christof Duffner
| Ski Jumping | Lillehammer | 1994 | Germany |

Christophe Capelle
| Cycling | Atlanta | 1996 | France |

Christoph Langen
Bobsleigh   Nagano   1998   Germany

Chris George
Baseball   Sydney   2000   USA

Christoph Sieber
Sailing   Sydney   2000   Austria

Christopher Fydler
Swimming   Sydney   2000   Australia

Christoph Langen
Bobsleigh   Salt Lake City 2002   Germany

Chris Pronger
Ice Hockey   Salt Lake City 2002   Canada

Chris Ahrens
Rowing   Athens   2004   USA

Chris Hoy
Cycling   Athens   2004   Great Britain

Christoph Bieler
Nordic C.   Turin   2006   Austria

Chris Hoy
Cycling   Beijing   2008   Great Britain

Chris Bosh
Basketball   Beijing   2008   USA

Christopher Zeller
Hockey   Beijing   2008   Germany

Christophe Kempe
Handball   Beijing   2008   France

Other British medallists:

SILVER:

Christopher Barton	Polo	Antwerp	1920
Christopher Baillieu	Rowing	Montreal	1976
Chris Mahoney	Rowing	Moscow	1980
Kris Akabusi	Athletics	Los Angeles	1984
Chris Hoy	Cycling	Sydney	2000
Chris Newton	Cycling	Athens	2004

BRONZE:

Kris Akabusi	Athletics	Barcelona	1992
Chris Boardman	Cycling	Atlanta	1996
Chris Newton	Cycling	Atlanta	1996
Chris Newton	Cycling	Beijing	2008

ACTING CHRISTOPHER

Chris Bisson (b. 1975) is a well-known face on British television, first appearing on screen as a teenager in 1990s' *Children's Ward*. He first came to national prominence playing the role of Saleem Khan in BAFTA award-winning British comedy *East is East* and went on to secure the part of womanising Vikram Desai in *Coronation Street*.

He played the work-shy brother of Nita for three years, leaving in 2002, and has subsequently played Kash Karib in Channel 4's *Shameless* and also appeared in the second series of *I'm a Celebrity, Get Me Out Of Here!*

The Blue Lagoon – the role he is best known for – launched the career of actor **Christopher Atkins** (b. 1961). Playing opposite Brooke Shields, the film caused controversy with its scenes of nudity (including both of the teenage stars) but has grossed almost $60 million since its release in 1980.

Mobbed by teenage female fans at the height of his fame – who literally tore the clothes off his back – he won several highly lucrative advertising contracts with the likes of Coca-Cola.

Playing the character Peter Richards, he had an affair with JR Ewing's wife, Sue Ellen, in the soap opera *Dallas*. He was nominated for a Golden Globe for his role in *The Blue Lagoon* but was also nominated for five Razzie Awards (awarded for a perceived lack of acting skills!) including Worst Actor of the Decade and Worst New Star of the Decade!

It was *That 70s Show* that first brought actor
Christopher Ashton Kutcher to the public's
attention and he has since starred in several successful
movies including *Dude, Where's my Car?*, *Just Married*
and *What Happens in Vegas...* The Iowa-born actor
has also starred and produced 64 editions of MTV's
flagship show *Punk'd* and he co-owns both an Italian
and Japanese restaurant in Atlanta and Los Angeles,
respectively.

He married actress Demi Moore in 2005 (fifteen years his
senior) and the pair are devout followers of the controversial
Kabbalah centre – a California-based organisation that
teaches a form of Jewish mysticism – also favoured by pop
star Madonna.

Christopher Allen Lloyd (b. 1938) is one of the
most recognisable faces in modern day cinema having
appeared in 64 films since making his cinematic debut as
a psychiatric patient in the classic *One Flew Over the Cuckoo's
Nest* in 1975.

He was a successful Broadway performer for many years
before breaking on to the big screen where his credits
have been wide ranging; from playing the eccentric 'nutty
professor' role of Emmett 'Doc' Brown in the *Back to the
Future* trilogy to arch villain Judge Doom in *Who Framed
Roger Rabbit*.

Other credits include:

Taxi (1978) – stealing the show as ex-hippie Reverend Jim
Ignatowski
Star Trek III: The search for Spock (1984)
The Addams Family (1991) – playing Uncle Fester
In Search of Dr. Seuss (1994)
The Simpsons Ride (2008)

Born in Boston, Massachusetts in June 1947, **Christopher
Allport** was a regular on US television in shows such as *The
X-Files*, *Matlock* and *ER*. In an article for the *Los Angeles Times*
in 2004 he wrote the prophetic words:

*"Any excursion into the mountains requires awareness. Have fun, but
be careful."*

In January 2008 he was one of three people killed when
three avalanches struck near the Mountain High ski resort
in Wrightwood, California.

Sheffield-born actor **Christopher Colquhoun** (b. 1970) is
most famous for his portrayal of womanising rogue Doctor
Simon Kaminski in BBC drama series *Casualty*. He also
played the same character in *Holby City* and has appeared in
The Bill and *Wire in the Blood*.

Christopher Bramwell was a familiar face on British television for almost two decades, appearing in such dramas as *Grange Hill* (playing Alan), *The Gentle Touch*, *Tales of the Unexpected*, *The Lion, the Witch and the Wardrobe* and *Van der Valk*. His most recent appearance was the role of Mr. Webb in *This Life*.

The maternal grandfather of actor **Christopher Plummer** was a former Canadian Prime Minister. As a youngster Plummer trained to be a concert pianist before developing a passion for the theatre and is best known for his role as Captain von Trapp in the 1965 film *The Sound of Music*.

He has also starred in a number of movie and TV films – over 250 to date. Winner of Broadway's Tony Award and American television's Emmy Award, he has also written for stage, concert halls and the small screen. His daughter, Amanda, has followed in her father's footsteps, appearing on Broadway and in several films including *Pulp Fiction* and *Battlestar Galactica*.

British actor **Christopher Mitchell** (1947-2001) played the role of Gunner Nigel 'Parky' Parkins in long running BBC sitcom *It Ain't Half Hot Mum*. He also made brief cameo appearances in *Only Fools and Horses*.

Welsh actor **Christopher Timothy** (b. 1940) is best known on British TV for his roles as vet James Herriot in *All Creatures Great and Small* and as Dr. Brendan 'Mac' McGuire in *Doctors*.

He has also provided the voice for numerous adverts by *The Sun* newspaper and played the role of announcer on the Kinks'1974 double album Preservation Act 2.

Christopher Frank Carandini Lee CBE was born in London in 1922 and has become one of the most recognisable actors in the history of moving pictures. He first rose to fame playing a variety of villainous roles, from Count Dracula in the Hammer Horror films to Francisco Scaramanga in James Bond film *The Man with the Golden Gun.*

He is perhaps best known for the role of Saruman in the *Lord of the Rings* trilogy which led to appearances in *Star Wars Episode II: Attack of the Clones* and *Star Wars Episode III: Revenge of the Sith.*

During the Second World War Lee served in the Royal Air Force and also worked as an intelligence officer in the Special Operations Executive, although all the actions of the SOE are still classified to this day.

Christopher Walken (born Ronald Walken in 1943) is a familiar face on TV and the big screen, having played a variety of roles in both mediums. He is the only man to have played a villain in both the James Bond and Batman franchises, taking the role of Max Zorin in *A View to a Kill* (1985) and Max Shrek in *Batman Returns* (1992).

In 2001 he was introduced to a new generation of fans when making a cameo appearance in Fatboy Slim's Weapon of Choice music video where he dances and flies around an empty hotel lobby in time to the music.

It won six MTV Awards in 2001. A little known fact about the New York actor is that he suffers from a genetic condition called heterochromia, meaning one of his eyes is blue and the other one brown.

The role of Superman in four feature films catapulted actor **Christopher D'Olier Reeve** to worldwide fame but he almost missed out on the part altogether as producers kept rejecting his CV.

His patience was rewarded and he underwent an intensive training schedule before the first film, which was supervised by former UK weightlifting champion David Prowse, the man in the Darth Vader suit in the *Star Wars* trilogy.

After the success of the first two Superman movies Reeve struggled to regain his former glories but this paled into insignificance with the events of May 27th 1995 when following a riding accident he suffered a spinal cord injury that left him paralysed from the neck down.

He became a high profile spokesman on the subject of spinal cord injuries and his work with the Christopher Reeve Foundation and the Reeve-Irvine Research Center has led to several multi-million dollar research programmes and benefited many people who have suffered the same fate that befell Reeve.

He made his directorial debut in 1997 and was nominated for a Golden Globe after directing and starring in a remake of the 1954 Hitchcock classic *Rear Window*. He died of a heart attack, aged 52, in October 2004.

—◆—

"CHOCS AWAY" CHRISTOPHER

Christopher Draper was a flying ace during World War I, earning the nickname 'the Mad Major' due to his penchant for flying under bridges! He rose to Squadron Commander – registering nine victories in dogfights – and became the first pilot to engage an enemy aircraft over London. He was awarded the DSC (Distinguished Service Cross) and the French Croix de Guerre (Cross of War) for his heroism.

He was the pilot of the first plane designed to specifically carry civilian passengers. Draper worked as a stunt pilot and acted in several films and during the 1930s he was as a double agent for MI6, feeding Nazi Germany false information.

When World War II began, Draper rejoined the RAF and commanded squadrons in West Africa and the Far East. In 1953 his protest at the treatment of war veterans reached a nadir when he flew along the Thames, under 15 of the 18 bridges.

He was arrested for his protest – being charged with flying too low in an urban area – and fined ten guineas. His memoirs *The Mad Major* were published in 1962 and he passed away, aged 86, in January 1979.

<hr>

WHAT A STINK CHRISTOPHER

In September 2007 a couple from Llanerchymedd, North Wales sued a local farmer for £50,000 after he dumped a 200-ton mountain of manure next to their garden!

Christopher Pedigrew and his partner, Deborah Lucas, commented that the smell even permeated their house when the windows were shut. They were seeking a nuisance injunction against dairy farmer, John Thomas, who dismissed their claims, commenting: "The southerly wind takes any manure smell away from their house."

<hr>

THE CHRISTOPHER COMMISSION

The **Christopher Commission** is the informal name for the Internal Affairs Department (AID) that effectively investigates all matters pertaining to the Los Angeles Police Department, such as civilian complaints and discipline procedures.

The commission was set up in July 1991 in the wake of the infamous beating of taxi driver Rodney King by several police officers in March of the same year. When the officers were controversially acquitted of his battery (despite a video tape showing the attack) in April 1992 it sparked the Los Angeles riots that lasted for several days and left 55 people dead, 2,383 injured and damage to 3,100 businesses.

The commission was initially led by **Warren Christopher** (who later became U.S. Secretary of State) and investigated all the complaints against police officers over a period of several years, eventually upholding only 2% of those complaints.

——⬥——

ARTISTIC CHRISTOPHER

Christopher 'Fangorn' Baker is a Birmingham-born artist who has enjoyed a successful career, as a cover artist as well as a storyboard and film conceptual artist; the pseudonym of Fangorn comes from a character in J.R.R.Tolkein's *Lord of the Rings*.

He is perhaps best known for his work as a concept artist in Tim Burton's film *Charlie and the Chocolate Factory* in 2005 although he also worked on Stanley Kubrick's *Eyes Wide Shut*.

New Zealand-born **Christopher Booth** (b. 1949) is a highly popular contemporary sculptor who studied at the University of Canterbury's school of fine arts. After graduating he has produced large, bold sculptures throughout his home land and as far away as North America and Europe.

Born in the New York borough of Manhattan and raised in the Bronx, **Christopher Aponte** is a classical ballet dancer who attended the famous High School of Performing Arts, upon which the movie *Fame* was loosely based.

His debut public performance came with the Delacorte Theater in Central Park and he has performed as principal dancer with the American Ballet Theatre, New York City Ballet and The Boston Ballet. He has also choreographed over 40 ballets and is best known for his interpretation of Ravel's Bolero.

Ohio-born automobile designer **Chris Bangle** (b. 1956) became the first ever American-born head of design at German car giants BMW. He was appointed to the role in 1992, after having designed the Z9 Gran Turismo concept car, and is now responsible for the BMW, Mini and Rolls Royce cars.

After rejecting his early idea of becoming a Methodist minister he instead attended the Art Center College of Design, based in Pasadena, California and gained his first employment in the automobile industry at Opel. He later moved to Italian company Fiat, working as chief designer of the Fiat Coupe.

LITERARY CHRISTOPHER

Author, poet and playwright **Christopher Marlowe** is
believed by many to have written several plays attributed to
Shakespeare. However, the Canterbury-born scholar's own
work was hugely popular in the 16th century with Marlowe
moving to London from Kent in 1587 when his *Tamburlaine
the Great* was adapted for the stage.

He later wrote *The Tragical History of Doctor Faustus* but at the
height of his powers, aged just 29, Marlowe was killed after
an altercation over a food bill turned violent.

Award-winning Irish author **Christopher Nolan** did not
let the considerable disability of cerebral palsy affect his
dream of becoming a writer. He first published a volume
of poems and short stories at the age of just 15 in 1981 and
wrote two critically acclaimed novels, the first of which,
Under the Eye of the Clock, being a third person autobiography
of his life, which won the Whitbread Prize in 1988.

In 1999 Chris – who wrote all his books with a pointer
that was attached to his head – published *The Banyan Tree*.
During his lifetime he received many honours including
Person of the Year in Ireland in 1988 and a Medal of
Excellence from the United Nations Society of Writers.

He passed away on February 20th 2009, aged 43, with Irish
politician Olivia Mitchell saying Nolan "was an inspiration
to millions and his influence will extend well beyond his
richly creative literary works".

Born in September 1968, Scottish fiction crime writer
Christopher Brookmyre has proven somewhat prolific,
with twelve titles since 1996:

Quite Ugly One Morning
Country of the Blind
~~*Not the End of the World*~~
One Fine Day in the Middle of the Night
Boiling a Frog
A Big Boy did it and Ran Away
The Sacred Art of Stealing
Be My Enemy (or F**k This For a Game of Soldiers)
All Fun and Games until Somebody Loses an Eye
A Tale Etched in Blood & Hard Black Pencil
The Attack of the Unsinkable Rubber Ducks
A Snowball in Hell

His quirkily titled books include several recurring characters
with investigative journalist Jack Parlabane most frequently
featured with Brookmyre's inspiration for the character
being Ford Prefect from Douglas Adams' *The Hitchhiker's
Guide to the Galaxy*.

His action-packed mix of politics, anti-establishment ethos,
social comment and strong storylines have made him one of
the most popular crime writers of his generation.

A *Time Out* review of *A Tale Etched in Blood* perhaps best
described his writing style:

"The kind of thing that Agatha Christie might have written
if she'd been off her tits on manky crack."

Although he lived the majority of his life in the US, novelist **Christopher Isherwood** spent his formative years in England after being born into an upper-class Cheshire family.

After shunning his background he lived an openly homosexual lifestyle in liberal Berlin in the 1920s and 1930s – his first book *All the Conspirators* being published in 1928.

His series of short stories entitled *Goodbye to Berlin* was published in 1939 and it is considered by many to be one of the greatest political works of the 20th century, later providing the inspiration for the musical *Cabaret*.

He emigrated to the US just before World War II, settling in Santa Monica, California where he worked as a teacher, wrote for Hollywood films and published a plethora of novels. He caused a Hollywood scandal when he started a relationship with 18-year-old artist Don Bachardy – thirty years his junior. The couple remained together for the rest of Isherwood's life, the writer dying at the age of 81, in 1986.

CHRISTOPHER MOVIE

The RKO feature film **Christopher Strong** (1933) featured a young Katharine Hepburn in only her second big screen appearance. She played Lady Cynthia Darrington, a free spirited record-breaking pilot, based upon pre-war U.S. flying heroine Amelia Earhart, who ensnares married MP Sir Christopher Strong.

On learning she is pregnant Lady Cynthia commits suicide in order to save Sir Christopher's political career and moral standing in upper class circles. The only female director to progress from silent movies to 'talkies', Dorothy Arzner was in charge behind the cameras and despite directing a series of relatively successful films in the inter-war years it would be Hepburn who would progress to real movie stardom, becoming one of the most recognisable faces in cinematic history.

—————◆◆◆—————

FASHION CHRISTOPHER

Born in England but brought up in Australia, **Christopher Essex** (1945-2006) was a costume and fashion designer who included the likes of Dionne Warwick, Phyllis Diller and Tina Turner amongst his clientele.

He opened his first salon, in Hong Kong, at a young age and worked for Bruce Lee. He later designed costumes for several stage shows, including *Little Shop of Horrors*, and Australian film *Strictly Ballroom*.

Yorkshire-born **Christopher Bailey** graduated from the Royal College of Art in 1994 and the fashion designer immediately started work as the womenswear designer at Donna Karan.

After two years his talents took him to Gucci, in Milan, where he stayed for five years before being appointed Creative Director at Burberry in 2001. He is now responsible for the overall image of the company; all advertising, art direction, store design and visuals, as well as having design input on all of the collections.

He was voted British Fashion Designer of the Year in 2005 and in November 2006 was awarded an honorary doctorate by the University of Westminster, from where he graduated in 1990.

Glasgow-born fashion designer **Christopher Kane** (b. 1982) rose to prominence in 2006 when he won the Harrods Design Award; part of the prize being his own showpiece window for two weeks at the famous London store.

He was immediately hired by Versace to work on the label's couture collection and in 2006 won both the best new British and best new Scottish designer of the year. He subsequently launched his own label – with his sister, Tammy – and also designed costumes for a Kylie Minogue music video.

ARCHITECT CHRISTOPHER

Sir Christopher Wren (1632-1723) was a highly influential scientist, mathematician and architect of the 17th century. He showed his academic prowess early in life and after attending Oxford University he was appointed Professor of Astronomy at Gresham College in London and then at Oxford University.

He was one of the founding members of the Royal Society, a collection of scientists and philosophers, which is still highly influential today. His first commission as an architect was a theatre in Oxford. Architecture then became his main focus.

The Great Fire of London in 1666 – which destroyed most of the city's medieval buildings – provided an opportunity for Wren to stamp his mark on the city and over the ensuing years 51 churches were constructed, plus his most famous building – St. Paul's Cathedral.

Put in charge of the design of all government buildings in 1669, he was knighted four years later. In addition to stamping his personality on London he was also responsible for many famous other structures including the Royal Observatory at Greenwich and Trinity College Library in Cambridge. He was buried in the graveyard at St. Paul's.

Born in Cambridge in 1820, architect **Christopher Crabb Creeke** had a huge influence in the early shaping of the Dorset seaside town of Bournemouth.

His skills as a draughtsman and town planner saw the area improve immensely during the time he was surveyor to the Bournemouth Commissioners – a body set up by Parliament in 1856 with a manifesto of improving the town and constructing a pier.

A bust of Creeke currently resides in the mayor's parlour while another depicted him sat on a toilet; homage to his success in constructing a drainage system for the town!

POSTIE CHRISTOPHER

A 5ft 5ins. postman from Sunderland, weighing less than 10 stone, was arrested after it was discovered that he had hoarded 13,819 letters and packages because he was not strong enough to deliver them!

Nineteen-year-old **Christopher Meek** started dumping sacks of mail at his home in September 2005, just a month into his job, and was rumbled when people started complaining that they had not received Xmas cards and gifts. He later admitted to opening over 1,500 items and stealing the contents, including DVDs, CDs and jewellery.

He was sentenced to four months in jail by Sunderland magistrates.

RAMSEY STREET CHRISTOPHER

Christopher Milne (b. 1950) played Philip Martin in
the popular Australian soap opera *Neighbours*. His first
appearance came in 1985 when he arrived as the new
manager of the Pacific Bank in Erinsborough, quickly
becoming romantically involved with employee Julie
Robinson.

However, at the time Philip was married – to his alcoholic
wife Loretta – and had two children, Michael and Debbie.
Eventually he decided to leave Loretta but changed his
mind when his daughter tried to commit suicide. In true
soap style a drunken Loretta was killed in a car crash, that
also temporarily paralysed Philip, and Julie became his
second wife.

The new family then left the soap, moving to the country, before
returning in 1992 with actor Ian Rawlings taking over the role.
Milne briefly returned to the show in 1998, playing Declan
Hewitt, and was back as Philip Martin in 2005 – his final
appearance coming in episode #4775 in July 2005.

Milne was also a major contributor to cult soap *Prisoner: Cell Block
H*, scripting numerous episodes and later wrote for *Neighbours*. In
recent years he has become a highly successful author of a series
of children's books entitled *Naughty Stories for Good Boys and Girls*,
which have sold over 350,000 copies worldwide.

THAT MUST HAVE HURT CHRISTOPHER

When **Christopher Coulter** and his wife, Emily, decided on a night of passion their evening took a somewhat bizarre twist which left him missing a rather vital organ!

The couple decided to spice up their love life by playing a few bondage games and Christopher decided to smear peanut butter on his private parts and let their Irish Setter, Ruby, lick it off.

Unfortunately for Christopher, Ruby got rather excited and ignored commands to let go so in desperation Emily threw a whole bottle of perfume over the dog. It broke over the dog and Christopher and the former was startled enough to let go, taking Christopher's manhood with her!

With Christopher unconscious his wife dragged him to their car – storing his missing part in an ice-cooler. After eight hours in surgery the doctors successfully re-attached the severed appendage as luckily the perfume that had drenched him, causing agonising pain, had helped to sterilise the wound and Christopher was rated as having an excellent chance of regaining full use.

The local animal welfare centre said they had no plans to seize Ruby and next time it will probably be dinner and a movie for the twosome… or should that be a threesome.

POLITICAL CHRISTOPHER

Chris Patten (b. 1944) served in government for thirteen years, holding a variety of posts including Minister for Overseas Development at the Foreign and Commonwealth Office and Secretary of State for the Environment.

He became responsible for the highly unpopular Poll Tax but was credited in 1992 as being the individual most responsible for engineering the Tories' unexpected general election win. Ironically he lost his seat in that election and was duly appointed the 28th, and last, Governor of Hong Kong.

Patten became a popular and charismatic governor – having an almost constant battle with the pro-Beijing political parties of Hong Kong – and was seen by the people as being on their side and was affectionately given his own Chinese name (Fat Pang).

After returning from the Far East he served as one of the UK's two representatives to the European Commission and in 2005 was raised to the peerage as Baron Patten of Barnes.

Before **Chris Mullin** (b. 1947) was elected as Labour MP for Sunderland South in 1997 he had worked for crusading ITV programme *World in Action*, helping to raise the plight of the Birmingham Six, jailed due to a miscarriage of justice in 1975 for pub bombings that killed 21 people under the banner of the IRA.

A strong believer in civil rights, Mullin has clashed with the government on several occasions and attained a reputation for campaigning on behalf of victims of injustice; he was one of the rebel Labour MPs that voted against the Government's proposal for a 90-day detention period without trial for terror suspects.

He announced in 2008 that he would not be standing at the next general election.

Christopher Andersen Hornsrud was Prime Minister of Norway for just one month in 1928.

He was the first Norwegian Labour Party Prime Minster and would remain a high powered political figure in the Scandinavian country for many years. He died at the grand old age of 100 years and 28 days in December 1960.

MUSICAL CHRISTOPHER

When **Christopher Martin** (b. 1977) and Jonny
Buckland met during Freshers week at University College
London – in September 1996 – they immediately began
planning to start a band and first played under the name of
Pectoralz.

It was not long before Guy Berryman and Will Champion
joined the pair and the quartet become known as Starfish.
During that period Martin and Champion tried to raise
some funds by busking at Covent Garden – playing Beatles
songs and The Bear Necessities from *The Jungle Book* – but
were moved on by the police after failing to generate any
income whatsoever!

Eventually a friend – Tim Rice-Oxley – permitted the band
to use the name of his group as he thought it sounded too
depressing so the newly named Coldplay started to gig
locally in the Camden area.

Incidentally, Rice-Oxley was subsequently offered the role
of keyboard player with the band but turned the offer down
as he was involved with a little known band called Keane…

The release of breakthrough single Yellow was followed
by the album Parachutes in 1999. In 2003 Martin married
American Oscar-winning actress Gwyneth Paltrow and
is now a high-profile supporter of Oxfam's Fair Trade
campaign whilst also being involved with Amnesty
International.

Singer **Christopher Davison** was born in Argentina
in 1948 – the son of an English diplomat – and spent his
childhood years in Malta, Nigeria and Zaire.

His family eventually settled in a 12th century castle in
Ireland – bought by his maternal grandfather Sir Eric de
Burgh – and it was from his mother's family that Chris de
Burgh would take his stage name.

His most famous song – Lady In Red – was believed by the
late Princess Diana to have been written about her but in
fact it was for de Burgh's own wife, Diane. His daughter –
Rosanna Davison – was crowned Miss World in 2003 and
in 2007 de Burgh became the first Westerner to play in Iran
since the 1979 revolution.

Born in Rotherham, South Yorkshire, **Christopher
Wolstenholme** moved to Teignmouth, Devon in 1989 and
started to drum for a post-punk band before being asked by
his friends, Matt Bellamy and Dominic Howard, to learn
the bass guitar and join their band The Rocket Baby Dolls.

He duly mastered the instrument and in 1994 the group
won a local battle of the bands contest. The shock at
winning the competition prompted the trio to quit their
jobs, forgo university, move away from home and change
their name to… Muse.

Their combination of alternative, hard rock, progressive
rock, electric and classical music saw the birth of the new
sub-genre of New Prog with Muse now having grown

into one of the UK's top music acts with an unrivalled reputation for spectacular stage shows.

Their most successful album to date, Black Holes and Revelations, lost out to Arctic Monkeys for the 2006 Mercury Music prize but Muse have won numerous other plaudits, including five MTV Europe Music Awards, five Q Magazine Awards, four New Musical Express Awards and two Brit Awards.

In June 2007 they were the first group to sell out the new Wembley Stadium, being watched by an aggregate crowd of 134,457 over two nights.

Born in Santa Barbara, California in May 1971, **Christopher Aubrey Shiflett** is the lead guitarist for post grunge band Foo Fighters. Joining the group after they held open auditions for the position, Shiflett first appeared on the Dave Grohl-led fourth album One By One.

In 2003 he was the founder member of punk band Jackson United, which counts his brother Scott in the line-up. Their self-titled EP was released on their own Magnificent Records label and debut album Western Ballads followed in 2004. Second album Harmony & Dissidence was released in 2008.

Christopher Allen Bouchillon (1892-1979) was a county blues artist from the U.S. state of South Carolina who is widely credited with introducing the 'talking blues' musical style. He formed the Bouchillon Trio, along with brothers Charlie and Uris, in the early 1920s and later recorded with his second wife, Ethel Waters, before retiring during the Great Depression of the 1930s.

His distinctive singing style was supposedly developed because of his terrible singing voice, which prompted his recording director to suggest he just talked on his records instead of singing! His first record with the new style was a hit and he has been credited by Bob Dylan as one of his greatest influences.

Best known as the lyricist of Squeeze, **Chris Difford** (b. 1954) penned such songs as Cool For Cats, Tempted and Up The Junction for the group while he has also provided words for the likes of Elton John, Jools Holland – his band mate in Squeeze – and Wet Wet Wet.

Middlesbrough-born **Chris Rea** (b. 1951) released eight albums in the 1980s with breakthrough single Stainsby Girls first bringing him to the attention of UK audiences, the song being a tribute to his wife, Joan, who attended Stainsby Secondary Modern School.

His album The Road To Hell saw Rea hit the number one spot in the UK. The success was repeated with follow-up album Auberge. After a serious bout of pancreatitis he returned to his blues roots, releasing several albums including the 2008 release The Return Of The Fabulous Hofner Blue Notes.

Lloyd Banks – born **Christopher Charles Lloyd** – is best known as a member of U.S. rap band G-Unit, along with childhood friend 50 Cent. When he released his first solo album in June 2004 it shot to the top of the American album chart, selling 443,000 copies in its first week of release.

Having appeared on four U.S. Billboard number one singles Ludacris – real name **Christopher Brian Bridges** – is one of the most successful recording artists in the U.S.

He has collaborated with such diverse acts as Good Charlotte, Alicia Keys and Kylie Minogue and after the release of his fourth album, The Red Light District, he formed The Ludacris Foundation, an organisation that helps high and middle school students motivate themselves in the creative arts.

In 2007 he appeared in the U.S. leg of Live Earth while he played himself in animated form in the 400th episode of *The Simpsons*, You Kent Always Say What You Want, first aired in May 2007.

OUTLAW CHRISTOPHER

Christopher Evans was the leader of the Evans-Sontang Gang
that robbed several trains in California between 1889 and 1892.
He was subsequently caught and became the first ever inmate
at Folsom Prison after being sentenced to life imprisonment. He
actually escaped from the facility, before being recaptured, and was
paroled in 1911 after becoming a 'model prisoner'.

CASUALTY CHRISTOPHERS:

Three actors have appeared in the BBC show since its 1986
inception:

Christopher Rozycki played the role of Kuba Trzcinski
between 1986 and 1988.
Christopher Guard was Ken Hodges in 1993.
Christopher Colquhoun took the role of Simon
Kaminski from 2002-2004.

MOXEY CHRISTOPHER

Best known for his role of Albert Arthur Moxey in hit TV
show *Auf Wiedersehen, Pet*, **Christopher Fairbank** has
been an instantly recognisable face on British TV for two
decades, being a regular in the original ITV series (1983-86)
along with Wayne, Dennis, Oz, Bomber, Barry and Neville.

He also appeared in the two series broadcast by the BBC between 2002 and 2004 and secured minor film roles in *The Fifth Element*, *Batman*, *Alien 3* and *Hamlet*. In addition his voice can be heard in Wallace & Gromit's *Curse of the Were-Rabbit* and as henchrat Thimblenose Ted in the 2006 animated British film *Flushed Away*.

⟹⟸

SOAPY CHRISTOPHER

Home & Away:

The popular Aussie soap can boast several actors and characters called Christopher including:

Actor	Character	
Chris Hemsworth	Kim Hyde	(2004-06)
Chris Foy	Woody	(2001)
Chris Mayer	Peter Sutherland	(2002)
Shaun Wood	**Christopher Fletcher**	(1993-98)
Dylan McGready	**Christopher Fletcher**	(1998-02)
Rian McLean	**Christopher Fletcher**	(2003)
Jason Clarke	**Christopher 'Kick' Johnson**	(2002)

EastEnders:

Petty small time criminal Charlie Cotton, played by **Christopher Hancock** (1928-2004), was part of Albert

Square for five years between 1986 and 1991. Charlie was a truly despicable character, forcing his wife to have an abortion just a year after their marriage, and continually leaving and returning to his long suffering spouse, Dot, who being a devout Christian always forgave him.

Even she was shocked, however, to learn that he had been having an affair with her half-sister, Rose, and that Charlie had committed bigamy when marrying Joan Leggett!

A long distance lorry driver, Charlie was killed in a road accident in 1991 but returned in 2000 when he played a ghost in *The Return of Nick Cotton* – a programme focusing on his son, Nick, whose evil reign on the soap included burglary, pimping, blackmail and murder… his dad would have been proud!

Other Christophers included:

Christopher Ettridge	Graeme	(2002)
Christopher Parker	Spencer Moon	(2002-05)
Christopher Reich	David	(1998-99)
Allan O'Keefe	**Chris Smith**	(1995-98)

Emmerdale Farm

Actor **Chris Chittel** has played the role of Eric Pollard in the popular show since 1986. Chittel plays a classic conman; a cheating swindler who has virtually no conscience. His legendary love life has resulted in five marriages:

1. Eileen probably wasn't too pleased when she discovered he had bigamously married his second wife!

2. Elizabeth was supposedly killed in 1993 when a plane hit Weatherfield although accusations persisted that Eric had done away with her!

3. He returned from the Philippines in 1997 with a sexy young bride. She left after becoming tired of Eric's dodgy business dealing and paranoia.

4. Gloria proved more conniving and power mad than Eric, encouraging him to sleep with a councillor to secure a mayoral nomination! She then disappeared only for Eric to receive a videotape showing a sun-drenched Gloria sipping a cocktail telling him she was glad to get rid of him!

5. Val was next but she stood against him in the local elections. At this point Eric got involved with the local dominatrix and played as dirty-as-possible to win power. The couple married at The Woolpack in June 2008.

Emmerdale character **Chris Tate** was played for 14 years by Peter Amory. He joined in 1989 when his father, Frank, and stepmother, Kim, bought Home Farm. He soon married Kathy but she was set to leave on the night of the plane crash episode where Chris was buried under the wreckage of The Woolpack.

He was left paraplegic and became bitter that Kathy was only staying with him because of his disability. She did eventually leave him when she found out he was having an affair and his mistress, Rachel, was pregnant with Chris' child!

They married in 1995 but after a year Rachel left, and then died. A third marriage – to former prostitute Charity Dingle – took place in 2001, although Chris was unaware that Charity had been having a lesbian affair with his sister, Zoe!

Charity was thrown out after Chris found she was 'keeping it in the family' by having an affair with her cousin Cain. After contracting a terminal illness he frittered away all his money so Charity would not inherit anything. He then arranged a meeting with his estranged wife, poisoned himself and framed Charity for his murder!

FIGHT FOR JUSTICE CHRISTOPHER

On November 2nd 1952 **Christopher Craig** and 19-year-old Derek Bentley broke into a Croydon confectionery manufacturer. The police captured Bentley first but when PC Miles climbed on to the roof he was shot dead by Craig, who was arrested when he fell on to a greenhouse from the roof, fracturing his spine.

Craig avoided the death penalty because he was under the age of 18 but Bentley, despite not having fired a shot, was found guilty of 'constructive malice' and sentenced to death.

An appeal – concentrating on the various ambiguities in the prosecution evidence, Bentley's low mental age of 11 and the fact that he was under arrest when his accomplice had fired the fatal shot – failed as the Home Secretary did not bow to pressure and Bentley was hanged on January 28th 1953.

Following his death there was great public unease and mainly through the work of his sister, Iris, a long campaign began to clear his name. He was granted a posthumous Royal Pardon and in July 1998 the Court of Appeal quashed his conviction for murder. Craig, who was imprisoned as a minor, was released after ten years, working as a plumber for the remainder of his life.

The story was told in 1991 film *Let Him Have It* with English actor **Christopher Eccleston** playing the role of Bentley. It was the first major role for Eccleston who became a household name in the UK after appearing in mid-1990s BBC drama series *Our Friends in the North*. He became the ninth incarnation of Doctor Who in 2005, playing the role for just one season, and has now appeared in 21 feature films.

COMBUSTABLE CHRISTOPHER

One Friday evening in March 1999, Hampshire resident **Christopher Piper** started drinking a crate of beer whilst smoking a few cigarettes. Told by his wife that he was literally 'playing with fire', he decided it would be an opportune moment to refill his butane lighter and, unsurprisingly, the increasingly inebriated Christopher spilled the fluid over his jumper.

His fascination with the lighter then saw him attempt to burn holes in his trousers and his knitwear literally went up in flames!

Instead of trying to smother the flames he decided to run from the house and try to beat out the flames with his hands – this action having the opposite effect of adding more oxygen to the fire, increasing the ferocity of the flames.

As he fled his curtains went up in flames and as he tried to extinguish the fire he managed to set a BMW ablaze. A neighbour attempted to put out the fire with towels but the fire was so hot that it burnt every part of his body, other than the soles of his feet, and soon after arriving at hospital he was pronounced dead with a verdict of accidental death recorded by the coroner.

FEMALE CHRISTOPHER

Although almost exclusively a male name, U.S. actress
Christopher Norris was the exception to the rule.
The New York-born thespian appeared in several movies
during the 1970s – including the 1975 disaster movie
Airport where she played a heroic air stewardess – and
later portrayed a soap 'vixen' in U.S. daytime show *Santa
Barbara*.

She has also appeared in such shows as *Matlock* (Homer's
sister-in-law's favourite), *Murder, She Wrote, Wonder Woman,
Happy Days* and *Fantasy Island*. A striking resemblance
to actress Melanie Griffith resulted in her more famous
double being interviewed by a somewhat confused
British press in the early 1990s about her role in the
Airport film!

GRIM REAPER CHRISTOPHER

Hapless **Christopher Kelly** lost his friends during a
night out in Morecambe, Lancashire in December 2007
and ended up in court after a catalogue of disastrous and
comical events.

The merry 31-year-old found himself in boggy sands and
lost his shoes, trousers and jacket when he freed himself.
Then, to escape the bitter cold, he climbed through an open
window in the town hall and took a camera and mobile
phone, attempting to call his mates on the latter.

He then soiled his underwear and had no option but to change into the only piece of clothing available – a Grim Reaper outfit complete with mask!

Captured by CCTV roaming the streets of Morecambe – missing only a scythe to complete his outfit – he decided to turn himself in to the police but then had to wait three hours for them to arrive!

His eventful night resulted in an appearance at Lancaster Magistrates' Court where it emerged that when he was arrested a probation officer laughed so much that he had to leave the proceedings!

Kelly pleaded guilty to burglary and received a six-month conditional discharge.

———⟫◆⟪———

VICTORIA CROSS CHRISTOPHER

These brave men received the VC, the highest and most prestigious medal awarded to British and Commonwealth forces for gallantry on the field of combat...

Christopher Furness
In May 1940 Lieutenant Furness engaged the enemy, against hopeless odds, in hand-to-hand combat in an attempt to aid the withdrawal of forty army vehicles from the French town of Arras.

His efforts forced the enemy to temporarily withdraw – allowing the vehicles to get through – but he was killed, aged 28, in the fighting.

Christopher Cox

Private Christopher Augustus Cox survived the horrors of the Great War (1914-18). He spent two years in the trenches, being wounded on the first day of the infamous Somme Offensive, and in March 1917, at Achiet-le-Grand, France, the stretcher-bearer with The Bedfordshire Regiment was pinned down in the trenches, along with his colleagues, under heavy artillery and machine gun fire.

However, Christopher went on to the field of fire and, single-handed, rescued four men from his battalion before helping to recover several wounded soldiers from an adjoining battalion. In the following two days he showed the same level of courage and for these acts was awarded the VC.

A serious foot injury saw him sent home in 1917 and he became father to eight children, and also had 14 grandchildren. On September 9th 2007 the Hertfordshire village of Kings Langley closed down for the day to celebrate the life of former resident Cox. A local woman was heard to say "he was the only man who could come back from Passchendaele and die falling from a ladder".

Sir Christopher Teesdale

Classed by many as the first 'modern war', the Crimean War was fought mainly in modern day Ukraine between the Russian Empire and an alliance containing the United Kingdom, France, the Ottoman Empire (Turkey) and the Kingdom of Sardinia.

It was in September 1855 that 22-year-old South African-born Lieutenant Teesdale volunteered to lead a counter-attack so fierce that it drove back the advancing Russian forces.

He then succeeded in inducing the Turkish artillerymen to return to their positions – from where they had been driven out – and later saved many wounded Russian soldiers from the wrath of the Turkish forces. His action won Teesdale the VC and he eventually rose to the rank of Major General of the Royal Artillery and was knighted by Queen Victoria in 1887.

<hr>

MAJOR LEAGUE BASEBALL CHRISTOPHERS

Christopher Britton	New York Yankees
Christopher Burke	Arizona Diamondbacks
Chris Bosio	Milwaukee Brewers and Seattle Mariners
Christopher Charles Dickerson	Cincinnati Reds
Chris Davies	Texas Rangers
Christopher Carlos Jones	Cincinnati Reds, Colorado Rockies and Arizona Diamondbacks
Cristy Mathewson	New York Giants and Cincinnati Reds

Chris Woodward	Toronto Blue Jays, New York Mets and Atlanta Braves
Chris Arnold	San Francisco Giants and Kintetsu Buffaloes
Christopher Coste	Philadelphia Phillies

WRESTLING CHRISTOPHERS

Christopher 'Chris' Chetti	The Rookie
Chris Adams	The Masked Avenger
Christopher Bauman	Chri$ Ca$h
Christopher Daniels	The Fallen Angel
Chris Wright	The Enforcer
Christopher Chavis	Tatanka
Chris Benoit	Pegasus Kid
Chris Jericho	Last Survivor
Chris Parks	Abyss
Chris Adkisson	Chris Von Erich

AUTHOR CHRISTOPHER

The pop-culture book *The Grilled Cheese Madonna and 99 Other of the Weirdest, Wackiest, Most Famous eBay Auctions Ever* was penned by U.S. author **Christopher Cihlar**.

The book examines, in detail, all the weird and wonderful items posted for sale on the internet auction site including the attempted sale by a woman of her virginity and a guy who was selling a damaged rake that he reckoned had been broken by a piece of debris that had fallen off the Space Shuttle Columbia!

Other crazy items included The Pope Mobile, Paris Hilton's lost dog signs, Britney Spears' pregnancy test and even the damaged front grill of Billy Joel's wrecked car!

Christopher Wood (b. 1935) is an English screenwriter whose credits include two James Bond movies – *The Spy Who Loved Me* and *Moonraker* – and a series of 'Confessions' books and screenplays under the pseudonym of Timothy Lea.

The British sex-farce movies starred Robin Askwith and Tony Booth and were widely criticised at the time as nothing more than softcore pornography.

It would be fair to say the films did not make the shortlists for an Oscar!

Confessions of a Window Cleaner (1974)
Confessions of a Pop Performer (1975)

Confessions of a Driving Instructor (1976)
Confessions from a Holiday Camp (1977)

In addition to his published work as Timothy Lea, Wood also wrote nine first-person perspective novels under the pen name of Rosie Dixon which ran along similar lines.

These titles included *Confessions of a Gym Mistress*, *Confessions from an Escort Agency*, *Confessions from a Package Tour* and *Confessions of a Lady Courier*. Ironically, the only Dixon book to not include the prefix of 'Confessions', *Rosie Dixon, Barmaid*, was the only one that was transferred on to the big screen in 1978 film *Rosie Dixon – Night Nurse*.

Writer **Christopher Bulis** is best known for his series of Doctor Who spin-off books, beginning with his 1993 published *New Adventure Shadowland*. He subsequently wrote five further books on the past adventures of the Doctor, under licence from Virgin Media, and penned a further five novels under licence from the BBC – his book *Vanderdeken's Children* being the only novel included in BBC Books' Eighth Doctor Adventures range.

Christopher Hampton CBE (b. 1946) has enjoyed a successful career as a playwright, screenwriter and film director. His first play *When Did You Last See My Mother?* was performed in the West End when Hampton was just 20 years old. He wrote four more plays before turning his attentions to screenwriting.

With over twenty screen credits to his name, Hampton won an Oscar in 1988 for Best Adapted Screenplay for *Dangerous Liaisons* and in 2007 he was nominated again for *Atonement*, starring Keira Knightley and James McAvoy.

———⟫◆⟪———

PRIVATE EYE CHRISTOPHER

With Richard Ingrams and Willie Rushton, **Christopher John Penrice Booker** founded satirical magazine *Private Eye*. He was the first editor in 1961 and, although replaced in 1963, has remained a regular member of the joke-writing collective.

In 1962 he was appointed as the resident political scriptwriter on landmark BBC satire show *That Was The Week That Was* and later contributed to *Spectator* magazine. In the 1970s he became an outspoken critic of the development of Britain's major cities, his scorn mainly reserved for concrete tower blocks.

He covered the Moscow Olympics for the *Daily Mail* in 1980, wrote a satirical column for the *Daily Telegraph* and replaced Auberon Waugh as weekly columnist for the *Sunday Telegraph*. In recent years Booker co-wrote several books on the effect on public life by bureaucratic regulation and specifically the role of the European Union. The titles provide a clue as to his opinion of the EU!

- *The Mad Officials: How the Bureaucrats are Strangling Britain* (1994)

- *The Castle of Lies* (1996)
- *The Great Deception* (2003)

His 2007 book *Scared to Death: From BSE to Global Warming, Why Scares are Costing us the Earth* analysed the effect of the 'scare phenomenon' on Western society.

———◆◆◆———

Mayflower Christopher

Born around 1570 in Harwich, Essex, **Christopher Jones** was the master of the famous *Mayflower*, which in 1620 transported the original Pilgrim Fathers from Plymouth, England to Plymouth, Massachusetts.

He became master of the *Mayflower* in 1609, owning a quarter of the vessel, and transported spices, wine and furs around the various colonies. His historic voyage across the Atlantic was the first act towards establishing the Plymouth Colony and he was honoured by the Pilgrims who named a river in nearby Kingston 'The Jones River'.

Also on board the ship was **Christopher Martin,** one of the forty-one Pilgrims, who hailed from the small village of Billericay and was a merchant by trade.

TERRORIST CHRISTOPHER

Christopher Caze (b. 1969) was one of France's most infamous terrorists. Originally a medical student he arrived back from a trip to Bosnia as a convert to Muslim fundamentalism and subsequently led a cell of mainly Algerian terrorists on a crime spree across France, robbing banks, armoured cars and general stores.

The group were eventually raided by the police after they had discovered a bomb inside a Peugeot that was parked just three blocks from the venue of the high powered G-7 meeting in 1996. Although Caze escaped that initial raid he was shot dead the following day as he tried to drive through a police checkpoint in neighbouring Belgium.

U.S.-born Paul Kenyatta Laws changed his name to **Christopher Paul** in 1994, after having received training from al-Qaeda in Pakistan and Afghanistan. He was charged by U.S. authorities, in April 2007, for conspiring to support terrorists, conspiring to use a weapon of mass destruction and providing support to terrorists.

As part of a plea bargain he pleaded guilty to all charges which carry a 20-year jail sentence.

ESPIONAGE CHRISTOPHER

Working in aerospace company TRW's 'Black Vault' (a classified communications centre), **Christopher Boyce** started receiving misrouted top secret CIA documents.

He claimed he was against their 'meddling' in other democratic countries – a sensational story in 1973 had uncovered a CIA plot that resulted in the Chilean president being overthrown and killed in a coup d'état.

Boyce decided against going public with the information so he stole classified documents concerning U.S. spy satellites and asked his friend Andrew Lee, a drug dealer (hence his nickname of 'The Snowman') to deliver the documents to the Soviet Embassy in Mexico City. His friend returned with a large stash of cash, which the duo split.

In 1977 he was arrested and received forty years in prison but incredibly his story did not end there. In January 1980 he escaped, and under the alias of Anthony Edward Lester robbed a total of 17 banks in Idaho and Washington State.

He was recaptured in August 1981 and released from prison on parole in 2002. Their story was the subject of Robert Lindsay's best selling 1979 book *The Falcon and the Snowman* (Boyce earning the Falcon tag due to his love of falconry).

Sir Christopher Curwen (b. 1929) was the head of the British Secret Intelligence Service (aka MI6) from 1985 until 1989 with a remit of carrying out espionage activities overseas – MI5 being concerned with security within the United Kingdom.

Between 1989 and 1991 Curwen was deputy secretary of the Cabinet Office and until 1998 served on the security commission, a body created in 1964 by Prime Minister Sir Alec Douglas-Home to investigate and report any security breaches in the Public Service.

———⟫◆⟪———

CROCODILE CHRISTOPHER

Animated children's cartoon **Christopher Crocodile** was first aired in 1993 and told the story of the friendly croc who left his native Mudagascar to help the people of Muddy Town – a place where it rains constantly, creating a very, very muddy place.

The arrival of Christopher was further bad news for the townsfolk but it was all good news for Christopher as he lounged around in the town's many mud pools, eating jars of peanut butter and custard.

However, it soon became obvious that Christopher was in fact an asset to Muddy Town as an eye for inventing various gadgets meant he could make life better for the rain-soaked residents.

STAR TREK CHRISTOPHER

Character **Christopher Pike** appeared in the very first pilot episode of *Star Trek* – entitled *The Cage*. Hailing from the city of Mojave, Pike was the first ever captain of the USS Enterprise.

A different actor portrayed the character when Pike re-appeared in a later *Star Trek* episode *The Menagerie*, although by this time James T. Kirk was in charge of the starship.

———⟐———

HITMAN CHRISTOPHER

Christopher Dale Flannery was a notorious Australian contract killer who was first arrested in August 1980 for the alleged slaying of barrister Roger Wilson but was unexpectedly acquitted.

Immediately re-arrested for the murder of Sydney brothel owner Raymond 'Lizard' Locksley, a jury failed to reach a verdict and he was acquitted at a second trial. He then moved to Sydney where he began working for crime figure George Freeman and in the mid-1980s became embroiled in the Sydney 'gang wars', refusing to stop the bloodbath despite local police trying to negotiate a ceasefire.

An eyewitness said that during a meeting with a high-ranking police officer, Flannery said: "You're not a protected species, you know – you're not a f**king koala bear."

In 1984 he was linked with the attempted murder of a drug squad detective and a year later Flannery's house was peppered with thirty shots. After escaping relatively unscathed he was alleged have completed a 'hit' on Tony 'Spaghetti' Eustace.

When police attempted to speak to the victim he used two rather choice words when asked who had shot him, dying a short while later!

Although Flannery's body has never been found it is alleged that he was actually killed in May 1985 by Sydney police who suspected that he was responsible for at least twelve contract killings...

<hr />

CREDIT CRUNCH WEDDING CHRISTOPHER

When **Christopher May** and Odette Fenwick were married in August 2008 their wedding day cost the princely sum of £480.

The couple, residents of Barnstaple in Devon, paid just £19 for the wedding rings and the remaining wedding essentials were gathered from a variety of sources, including the internet, charity shops and bargain rails.

The bride and groom held their reception at the engineering plant where Christopher worked and were given a momento of their big day as the BBC *Money Programme* filmed the nuptials.

The pair agreed that it did not matter that the wedding had a bargain basement cost and saved more money on their honeymoon – they did not have one!

<hr>

KENNEDY CHRISTOPHER

Born in July 1963, **Christopher Kennedy** was the eighth child to Robert F. Kennedy and Ethel Skakel. Within a few months of becoming a Kennedy his famous uncle, JFK, was assassinated in Dallas, Texas and tragically for Christopher his father was mortally wounded in June 1968 after being shot several times in Los Angeles whilst celebrating his victory in the California Democratic presidential primary.

Thankfully Christopher has so far survived the legendary 'Kennedy curse' which has claimed a multitude of victims over 65 years. The trail of disaster includes:

1941   Rosemary Kennedy undergoes a frontal lobotomy after her increasingly violent behaviour and mood swings.

1944   Joseph Kennedy dies in a mid-air plane crash over the English channel while flying a bombing mission during World War II.

1948   Kathleen Kennedy Cavendish dies in a plane crash in France.

1955   Jackie Kennedy, wife of JFK, suffers a miscarriage.

1963   Patrick Kennedy, son of JFK and Jackie, is born six weeks premature and dies two days after birth.

JFK is assassinated on the same day, November 22nd, that his great grandfather dies.

1964   Ted Kennedy is pulled from the wreckage of a plane crash in which his aide and the pilot were both killed. He spends weeks in hospital recovering from multiple injuries.

1968   Bobby Kennedy is assassinated in L.A.

1969   The family is engulfed in scandal from the 'Chappaquiddick incident' when a car driven by Ted Kennedy goes off a bridge, killing his passenger, Mary Jo Kopechne.

1972   Christopher's brother, Joseph Kennedy, is on a Lufthansa jet over India when it is hijacked by five Palestinians and diverted to Yemen.

1973   Step-son to Jackie Kennedy, Alexander Onassis, dies in a plane crash.

1974   Ted Kennedy Jnr. loses his leg to cancer at the age of just 12.

1984   Another of Christopher's siblings, David, is found dead in a Palm Beach motel after a drug overdose.

1988   Christina Onassis, Jackie Kennedy's stepdaughter, is found dead in Argentina after a heart attack brought on by drug abuse.

1997   Michael Kennedy, son of Bobby, is killed in a skiing accident in Aspen, Colorado.

1998   JFK's son, his wife and her sister are all killed when a private plane piloted by John crashed into the Atlantic Ocean.

2008   Ted Kennedy is diagnosed with a brain tumour after being hospitalised in Massachusetts.

LOOSE CHANGE CHRISTOPHER

Christopher Ironside OBE was an English-born designer and painter who first came to public attention when his decorations adorned Pall Mall, in London, during the 1953 coronation of Queen Elizabeth II.

However, he is best known as the designer of the reverse side of the present fifty, ten, five, two and one pence coins, as well as the defunct halfpenny. He has also designed various commemorative coins issued by the Royal Mint and also coins for Tanzania and Brunei.

———⇒◆⇐———

MULDER & SCULLY CHRISTOPHER

The creator of the hugely popular U.S. programme *The X-Files*, **Christopher Carter** was born in California in 1956, graduating from Long Beach University after majoring in journalism.

After winning a plum job at Walt Disney Pictures he subsequently started his own production company in 1983 called Ten Thirteen Productions. The name is derived from his birthday of October 13th and the company has produced all 202 episodes of the TV series, plus two feature films and various spin-offs. Carter has been credited with a variety of roles including creator, writer, producer and director.

MINTED CHRISTOPHER

Telecommunications entrepreneur **Christopher Bradbury** was a new entry in 2007 on the *Sunday Times* list of the wealthiest people in the UK. His estimated fortune of £70m has been generated through the running of premium rated phone-in lines and text-based dating services.

He started out selling hardware to the phone line operators but set up his own company in 1994 and is hot on the heels of the UK's richest telecoms entrepreneur, Richard Branson, who is just a mere £2.5 billion ahead!

New Zealand-born **Christopher Chandler** generated the majority of his huge $1.7 billion wealth through the investment company, Sovereign Global, which he ran with his brother, Richard, until 2006.

His new company has invested greatly in beverage and financial services in India. He is also a great advocate of social investment having launched a $50m venture in 2008 to help entrepreneurs in the developing world.

His personal fortune puts Chandler in 707th place in Forbes' list of the world's wealthiest billionaires.

Chris Wright co-founded the Chrysalis record label in the late 1960s. The label (the name derives from an amalgam of the two founder members surnames) made history when releasing the world's first 'video album' in 1979, Blondie's Eat To The Beat.

Their offshoot label, 2Tone Records, championed the sound of ska and reggae music with acts Madness and The Specials triggering a new wave of music in the UK.

At the start of the 1980s Chrysalis was at the forefront of the British New Romantic movement with Spandau Ballet and Ultravox.

The label was sold to EMI and Chris concentrated on a new portfolio, including record publishing, television and radio. Most were subsequently sold and he returned full circle – running a music publishing business that includes David Bowie. A sports enthusiast, Wright was chairman of Queens Park Rangers for five years but put the club into administration in 2001, personally costing Wright a reported £15m.

He duly bought Wasps rugby union club and the Stratford Place racing stud in Cheltenham. His personal wealth is estimated at over £95m.

At the 2008 RM auction of classic Ferraris – held annually at the Ferrari factory in Maranello, Italy – the star lot of a 1961 250GT SWB California Spyder attracted fierce bidding from two collectors, pushing the bidding well above the guide price of £2m.

However, the two rivals were blown away when British DJ **Chris Evans** made his one and only offer – an astonishing €6.45m. Suffice to say he added the car, which was once owned by Hollywood actor James Coburn, to his growing collection and paid a new world record sum for a motor vehicle sold at auction.

———◆———

BLUE PETER CHRISTOPHER

Christopher Trace (b. 1933) is best known for being the first presenter of BBC's children's show *Blue Peter*. The programme first aired on October 16th 1958 and Trace would remain with the show for almost nine years before a *Blue Peter* summer visit to Norway proved his downfall.

In Scandinavia, Trace had an affair with a 19-year-old receptionist and after his wife filed for divorce the BBC – the 1960s explosion of freedom and tolerance had yet to reach Auntie Beeb – forced his resignation. He lost a large amount of his own money in a failed film company and filed for bankruptcy in 1973.

He lost two toes in an accident at the engineering company where he had become general manager and the factory closed down on one day in 1978 so the workforce could watch Trace back on *Blue Peter* when the show celebrated its 20th anniversary.

His lasting legacy to British language is without doubt the two phrases he coined whilst on the show; 'And now for something completely different' – a phrase hijacked in the 1970s by Monty Python – and 'Here's one I made earlier', which is still heard regularly on various shows on UK television.

The son of a former British ambassador to Central American country El Salvador, **Christopher Wenner** (b. 1954) first appeared as a *Blue Peter* co-presenter on September 14th 1978 and remained with the show until leaving, by mutual agreement, in June 1980.

He left to concentrate on a career in journalism and in 1985, while reporting the problems in Beirut, he disappeared for 18 days before re-appearing safe and well. He was also at the sharp end of civil unrest in Serbia in 1998 when he was attacked by angry civilians during protests. He survived and now runs his own production company.

⋘━◆━⋙

CYCLING CHRISTOPHER

Scotsman **Sir Chris Hoy MBE** entered Olympic history in August 2008 when he became the first British athlete in 100 years to win three gold medals at one games.

He matched the record of swimmer Henry Taylor, from the London games in 1908, and took his personal tally to four after having also struck gold in Athens four years earlier. After winning both the team sprint and keirin – a track cycling event in which racing cyclists sprint for victory – he beat team-mate Jason Kenny in the individual sprint to complete a hat-trick of gold medals.

The success capped a medal-laden career for Hoy, which began in 1999 when he won a silver medal at the World

Championships. He won a further eight gold, one silver and two bronze medals at subsequent World Championships while also winning a silver at the 2000 Sydney Olympics and two gold and a bronze medal at the Commonwealth Games.

He received an MBE in 2005 and is now firmly established as the greatest cyclist the UK has ever produced.

Prior to the emergence of Hoy, the British Olympic hopes rested with **Chris Boardman** (b. 1968) who won a 4000m individual pursuit gold at the Barcelona games in 1992 and a bronze in the individual time trial in Atlanta four years later.

Nicknamed *the Professor*, due to his meticulous attention to detail, Boardman was famous for the specially-designed carbon-fibre bike, created by UK sports car company Lotus, which he rode to several medals.

He later took part in the blue riband event of road racing – the Tour de France – and wore the yellow jersey on three occasions.

Surely his greatest success was being name-checked by Del Boy in *Only Fools and Horses* when he tried to sell some dodgy cycle helmets!

BOBSLEIGH CHRISTOPHER

As part of the four-man bobsleigh team, **Charles 'Christopher' MacKintosh** won a gold medal for Britain in the 1938 World Championships, held in the Bavarian town of Garmish-Partenkirchen.

In addition to the bobsleigh, MacKintosh competed for Britain in several other events, including rugby union and skiing, and finished in sixth place in the men's long jump at the 1924 Olympic Games in Paris.

MOBILE TROUBLE CHRISTOPHER

When **Christopher Walker** decided to send a sleazy video call to his girlfriend's mobile phone he ended up in hot water after dialling a total stranger 500 miles away by mistake!

The Scotsman, who was off work at the time and had been drinking, accidentally sent the X-rated video to a young lady in Devon who was somewhat taken aback when the nether regions of an unknown male appeared on her mobile phone!

Walker pleaded guilty at Stirling Sheriff Court, in September 2008, to conducting himself in a disorderly manner, sending an explicit video and committing a breach of the peace.

"SHIVER ME TIMBERS" CHRISTOPHER

Englishman **Christopher Condent** was reputed to be one of the most bloodthirsty pirates who ever set sail. One story tells of a journey he made across the Atlantic which reached a crisis point when an Indian member of the crew – who had been badly mistreated on the voyage – threatened to set fire to the ship's gunpowder stash.

Condent quickly quelled the uprising by shooting the man in the face. His crew then hacked his body to pieces and the gunner slashed open his stomach, tore his heart out and boiled it for his tea! During his travels he captured many ships including a Dutch warship that he kept and renamed *The Flying Dragon*, before proceeding to terrorise the coasts of Brazil and later Africa.

In lighter moments he was rather partial to torturing his Portuguese prisoners by cutting their ears and noses off!

Around 1720, near Bombay, India, his crew captured an Arabian ship laden with treasures with an estimated value of £150,000 – an astronomical sum almost three centuries ago.

This huge haul effectively broke up the pirates and Condent eventually married the sister-in-law of the governor of the French colony island of Reunion.

Eighteenth century pirate **Christopher Moody** was known for his policy of 'no quarter' – in contemporary English this meant that no prisoners were taken alive!

He terrorised the coast of North and South Carolina for a period of five years, flying his distinctive Jolly Roger flag which instead of being a white skull and cross bones on a black background was in fact gold on red. He also added a couple of extra motifs that left no seafaring individual in any doubt that if he came across Moody it would in all probability be their last breath!

He was eventually captured and hanged at modern-day Cape Coast in Ghana.

⇒◆⇐

LITERARY CHRISTOPHER

American writer **Christopher Peter Andersen** (b. 1949) honed his literary skills at the likes of *Time Magazine*, *Vanity Fair* and *The New York Times*. However, he is best known for his controversial and highly popular biographies of famous public figures, having published the following books which flew off the shelves in the US:

The Kennedy Family	*Jack and Jackie: A portrait of an American marriage* *Jackie after Jack* *The Day John died* *Sweet Caroline*
The Royal Family	*The Day Diana died* *Diana's boys* *After Diana*

U.S. Presidents	*Bill and Hillary: The marriage*
	American Evita
	George and Laura: Portrait of an
	American marriage
Barbra Streisand	*Barbra: The Way She is*
Madonna	*Madonna: Unauthorised*

———⟫•◈•⟪———

THE PURSUIT OF HAPPINESS CHRISTOPHER

The inspirational life story of **Christopher Paul Gardner** (b. 1949) proved a worldwide box office hit after being released in December 2006, grossing an astonishing $500m.

Will Smith took the lead role of a heart-warming film that told the story of single parent Gardner's desperate struggles in the 1980s as he battled against poverty and homelessness; Smith's own son, Jaden, portrayed the role of Gardner's son in the movie.

Although the big screen version did condense many events in Christopher's life into a short timescale, the basic facts rang true as he overcame adversity to become a multi-millionaire whose philanthropic work has included schemes for low-income housing in San Francisco – where he was once homeless himself – and to ensure the well-being of children.

When the movie was released it was reported that Gardner believed Will Smith to have been miscast in the role. However, Gardner's daughter, Jacintha, soon corrected her father when commenting: "If Smith can play Muhammad Ali, he can play you", referring to a previous film in which Will Smith had portrayed the great boxer.

⟫◆⟪

POKER CHRISTOPHER

Professional poker player **Chris Ferguson** has made a handsome living out of the game after graduating from UCLA in 1999 with a Ph.D. in computer science. Both his parents have doctoral degrees in mathematics and Chris' approach to poker relies heavily on maths, in addition to game theory and writing his own computer simulations.

A player since the age of 10, he recorded his first big win in 2000 when walking off with the $1.5m first prize in the World Series of Poker. His nickname of Jesus – due to his long hair and beard – is somewhat ironic, as he is an atheist.

His total tournament winnings now exceed a staggering $7.3m!

MURDEROUS CHRISTOPHER

Florida-born **Christopher Pittman** hit the headlines in 2005 when he was convicted of the murder of his grandparents, when aged just 12 years old, in November 2001.

His defence claimed he acted under the influence of prescription anti-depressant drug Zoloft but the jury decided otherwise, sentencing the teenager to 30 years in the State Penitentiary.

Christopher J. Newton stated that he only burgled his father's house so he could return to prison and his state of mind was called into question again in 2001 when he decided he wanted to die in prison.

To facilitate this wish he committed the aggravated murder of his cellmate, Jason Brewer, stating at the time that he had become frustrated at his cellmate's poor chess-playing skills!

He duly received the death penalty in 2001 and in May 2007 was involved in one of the most bizarre executions in U.S. history – due to his size (he weighed 265 pounds) it was extremely difficult to find a vein in which he could receive his lethal injection.

Incredibly, the process took so long that Newton was given a bathroom break during the proceedings. Two hours later, and after ten attempts, he was executed in the Southern Ohio Correctional Facility.

OH, YOU MEANT THAT CHRISTOPHER

Christopher doubles:

1. Chris Walker	English motorcycle racer who lists his worst feature as his love of puddings.
2. Chris Walker	Member of the GB squash team that won the World Championship in 1995 and 1997.
3. Chris Walker	Northern Irish footballer who has the Glentoran club crest tattooed on his chest.
4. Christopher Walker	The real name of comic book hero 'The Phantom'.
5. Chris Walker	Australian rugby league player.

1. Chris Taylor	Cricketer who has appeared for Yorkshire and Derbyshire.
2. Chris Taylor	NFL running back for the Houston Texans American Football team.
3. Chris Taylor	Anglo-American journalist who writes for *Time Magazine*.
4. Chris Taylor	Character played by Charlie Sheen in the movie *Platoon*.
5. Chris Taylor	Wrestler who holds the record of the heaviest ever Olympian, set at the 1972 Munich games, where weighed 412 pounds (187kg). He died of a heart attack at the age of only 29.

DISC JOCKEY CHRISTOPHER

Born in 1882, **Major Christopher Reynolds Stone**
is widely regarded as the UK's first DJ. While serving in
the Royal Fusiliers he became editor of *The Gramophone*
magazine and approached the BBC himself with the idea
of hosting a record-based programme.

The Beeb somewhat looked down their nose at popular
culture but Christopher eventually persuaded them and on
July 7th 1927 he started to play records on air. A sign of the
times was that he wore a full dinner jacket when presenting
but his style – a marked contrast to the formal presentation
in vogue – made him a hugely popular figure and he stayed
for seven years before joining commercial station *Radio
Luxembourg.*

He presented the first children's radio show, *Kiddies Quarter
Hour*, on Radio Lyons but caused a stink in 1941 when, after
rejoining the BBC, he wished the King of Italy a happy
birthday – Britain was at war with the Italians and the station's
controller was sacked after the scandal.

An avid record collector, Stone was praised for his ground-
breaking work by fledgling music magazine *Melody Maker* in 1957.

"Everyone who has written, produced or compared a
gramophone programme should salute the founder of his trade."
Leeds-born **Chris Moyles** (b. 1974) joined local station
AIRE FM where one of his responsibilities was to make
cups of tea for future *Countdown* star Carol Voderman!

He moved abroad to work for Radio Luxembourg, using his mother's maiden name of Holmes. After the station closed, he worked for a wide variety of stations in Bradford, Stoke and Bristol.

After developing his own inimitable style his profile rose considerably when he began presenting 'The Late Bit' on London's Capital FM in 1996. His on-air antics gave Moyles a cult following; he once painted a female guest's breasts on air and regularly cut off and abused boring callers.

He is credited with introducing Oasis to southern listeners and before long he became the second youngest-ever DJ (after Noel Edmonds) on BBC Radio 1. Starting on July 28th 1997, Moyles became the self-styled 'saviour of early morning radio' and such was his popularity that he moved on to the Saturday morning show in 1998, running such features as Girls Going to Football and May Divorce be With You.

DJ Christopher Moore was the first voice heard when pioneering offshore radio ship Radio Caroline first broadcast on Easter Sunday 1964.

"This is Radio Caroline on 199, your all-day music station" announced Moore before playing Not Fade Away by the Rolling Stones. The BBC and Radio Luxembourg now had a serious competitor and commercial radio in the UK would never be the same again.

GUNPOWDER PLOT CHRISTOPHER

The night of November 5th is now a popular date on the English calendar and it was Yorkshire-born **Christopher 'Kit' Wright** who indirectly had a hand in creating what is now known as 'Bonfire Night'.

He conspired along with the likes of Guy Fawkes and his brother, John, in the infamous Gunpowder Plot of November 1605 when a group of English Roman Catholics unsuccessfully attempted to blow up Westminster Palace and kill King James I.

Wright hailed from a strict Roman Catholic family – his parents were imprisoned for a total of 14 years for their beliefs – and was actually a school friend of Fawkes in York. When the plot was uncovered the conspirators fled. On November 8th 1605, at Holbeach House in Staffordshire, the men of the Sheriff of Worcester surrounded them.

In the ensuing battle an explosion of gunpowder killed some of the group and during the immediate aftermath the sheriff's men stormed the building and Wright, Thomas Percy and Robert Catesby were shot dead.

GERMAN TOWEL CHRISTOPHER

When cruise ship captain **Christopher Wells** put a 20-minute limit on reserving sunbeds on his 77,000-ton P & O Oceana liner he whipped up a storm of controversy, in particular from the German passengers.

The captain announced "We don't want that kind of Germanic behaviour" but was reported to the Equality and Human Rights Commission by several people and was forced to issue a full, unreserved apology to passengers.

The captain, who is married to a German, was soon promoted to the command of the Queen Mary 2, although the two events are not believed to be connected!

⟫◆⟪

SERIAL KILLER CHRISTOPHER

Known as 'The Beauty Queen Killer', Australian-born **Christopher Wilder** terrorised America in 1984, kidnapping and raping at least ten women and killing at least seven.

After emigrating to the U.S. in 1969, Wilder was constantly appearing in court for various sexual misdemeanours; in 1980 he raped a teenage girl but escaped a jail sentence, receiving five years' probation and therapy instead.

On a visit home in 1982 he kidnapped two 15-year-old girls but after his parents lodged the $350,000 bail Wilder returned to the U.S. to await a trial date. He never returned.

His killing spree is believed to have started in February 1984 with Rosario Gonzalez and Elizabeth Kenyon. Neither girl's bodies were ever found but the net was starting to tighten around Wilder and he fled.

He quickly killed again and went on a spree of violence that took him across several southern US states. After killing 17-year-old Michelle Korfman in Las Vegas, Wilder was placed on the FBI's 'Ten Most Wanted' list.

His reign ended on April 13th 1984 when he was shot dead by police. Although only officially credited with eight murders, it is widely believed he has killed almost three times that number.

FOUR-MINUTE MILE CHRISTOPHER

Sir Christopher Chataway was one of two pacemakers for Roger Bannister when he became the first man in history to run a sub-four minute mile in May 1954. Chataway was an outstanding athlete in his own right. Only terrible luck in the final of the 5,000 metres at the 1952 Helsinki Olympic Games denied him a certain medal; he was leading three other competitors around the final bend but fell, finishing in fifth place.

He did win a silver medal in the distance at the 1954 European Championship and set a new world record time – 13 minutes, 51.6 seconds – at White City, London. The same year he became the inaugural winner of the BBC's Sports Personality of the Year and retired after competing in the 1956 Olympics.

Whilst working for Guinness it was Chataway who recommended his old university pals – Norris and Ross McWhirter – when his employer floated the idea of the *Guinness Book of Records*.

After a short TV career he moved into politics, winning a seat as MP for Lewisham North in 1959. He has been President of the Commonwealth Games Council of England since 1990 and was knighted in 1995.

IMPOSTER CHRISTOPHER

When French-born **Christophe Rocancourt** (b. 1967) faked the deeds to a Paris property, subsequently netting $1.4m from its sale, it was the start of a career as a con artist and impostor that, it is estimated, netted him $40m. After moving to the United States he convinced many affluent people that he was a French member of the famous Rockefeller family, conning his victims to invest large sums of money in his various schemes.

Part of his masquerade was to always have a beautiful woman on his arm; he married Playboy model Pia Reyes and, incredibly, at one point also lived with another Playboy model, Rhonda Rydell!

During his time in the fast lane he maintained the pretences of being a movie producer, ex-boxing champion and venture capitalist and was so convincing that he became friends with several high profile celebrities, including Mickey Rourke and Jean-Claude Van Damme.

Eventually, he fell foul of the authorities and after jumping bail he fled across the border to Canada, writing a sensational book in 2002 that ridiculed his many unfortunate victims.

He was extradited back to the U.S. and was charged with theft, grand larceny, smuggling, bribery, perjury and fraud! He was fined an astonishing $9m, ordered to pay $1.2m in restitution and sentenced to five years behind bars.

MISCARRIAGE OF JUSTICE CHRISTOPHER

When the unfortunately named **Christopher Slaughterford** was executed for the murder of Jane Young at Guildford on July 9th 1709 it brought an end to a series of events that had almost certainly brought the English legal process into disrepute.

A miller by trade, Slaughterford was effectively engaged to Miss Young but when she mysteriously disappeared in October 1703 local suspicions pointed to Christopher. When her lifeless body was found, a month later, Christopher was virtually pronounced guilty by the locals and decided to surrender himself to the authorities.

Two magistrates subsequently discharged him before a third sent him to trial for the crime where he was duly acquitted and released. However, the 'Chinese whispers' of his peers led to a sum of monies being raised so an appeal could be launched against the verdict.

Incredibly, at the second trial, despite a new jury having the same evidence, he was pronounced guilty and sentenced to death! A little known English law meant that he could not receive a royal pardon because he had been found guilty on appeal – the authorities considered the case dubious and would certainly have granted him his freedom.

He therefore went to the gallows pleading his innocence despite evidence emerging that Jane Young had been seen in the company of an ex-convict on the night of her disappearance. A witness had unbelievably testified that he had come across the pair on a common at 3am and soon after heard a shrieking sound, like the voice of a woman!

Clearly this testimony was not considered crucial in his case…

⟫◆⟪

SUNDRY CHRISTOPHERS

Christopher Black
Criminal lawyer and political activist.

Christopher Moltisanti
A character in television series *The Sopranos*.

Chris Quinten
Actor who played Brian Tilsley in *Coronation Street* from 1978 to 1989.

Kit Carson
American frontiersman.

Chris Lowe
One half of UK band Pet Shop Boys.

Chris Squire
Bassist for UK prog rock group Yes.

Chris Stine
Founder member of American pop act Blondie.

Christopher Cross
Texan singer-songwriter who is the only individual to win all of the 'Big Four' U.S. Grammy Awards (best record, song, album and new artist) in the same year, 1979.

Best known for his songs Ride Like the Wind, Sailing and Arthur's Theme (Best That You Can Do).

Christopher Cross Griffin
Character in U.S. animated series *Family Guy*. Like his father, Chris is obese and has a low IQ with little or no common sense.

Christopher Rouse
U.S. film editor who won an Oscar for Best Editing for 2007 film *The Bourne Ultimatum*.

Kris Kristofferson
U.S. singer and actor who has released over twenty albums and appeared in over seventy movie and TV roles.

Chris Adams
Talented right-handed batsman who represented his home county of Derbyshire before moving to captain Sussex, announcing he was stepping down from the role in September 2008 after leading his side to the Pro40 Division One title.

He has also appeared for England in five Test matches and five One-Day Internationals.

Christopher Gunning
Award-winning British composer who won a BAFTA in 2007 for his film score to *La Vie En Rose*.

Christopher Hughes
Winner of *Mastermind* (1983), *International Mastermind* (1983) and *Brain of Britain* (2005).

Chris Eubank
Eccentric former WBO middleweight boxing champion who is now more known for driving around in a huge American Peterbilt truck cab (the largest truck in Europe), dressing as a stereotypical English gent (complete with jodhpurs and monocle), and appointing his own town crier after buying the title of the Lord of the Manor of Brighton.

Christopher Cazenove
English actor who played Ben Carrington in American soap *Dynasty* between 1985 and 1987. Educated at Eton College, he is often cast as a British aristocrat while he has appeared on several occasions in popular British TV legal drama *Judge John Deed*.

Christopher Ellison
Played DCI Frank Burnside in the popular TV detective series *The Bill* and is a fan of Brighton & Hove Albion FC.

Christopher Biggins
British comedy actor who won ITV's *I'm a Celebrity Get Me Out of Here!* in 2007 and appeared in 1970s comedy classics *Some Mothers Do 'Ave 'Em* and *Whatever Happened to the Likely Lads*.

He is also remembered for his part of supermarket manager, Adam Painting, in children's show *Rentaghost*.

────◆────

COMMENTATOR CHRISTOPHER

The dulcet tones of **Christopher Martin-Jenkins** (b. 1945) can be regularly heard on Test Match Special (TMS) on BBC Radio 4. Known as CMJ, he moved to radio in 1973, joining the legendary Brian Johnston, and has remained a familiar voice to cricket followers ever since.

As well as being cricket correspondent for the BBC for a total of thirteen years, he has also worked for the *Daily Telegraph* (1990-99) and *The Times* before former Test captain Michael Atherton replaced him as the Times' chief cricket correspondent in May 2008.

He also wrote the *Complete Who's Who of Test Cricketers* while his son, Robin, has played in almost 200 first-class games for Sussex County Cricket Club.

────◆────

ENGLISH CHRISTOPHER

When **Christopher Molyneux** completed his census form in 2001 he refused to answer the question: 'What is your ethnic group?'

The form provided spaces for Scottish, Irish and various Asian groups but not English so the Cheshire design consultant refused to tick the only box available – British. The proud Englishman twice sent back the form with letters of protest but eventually was prosecuted by the Office for National Statistics, which carried a possible maximum fine of £1,000.

He was eventually fined £150 including costs but a disgruntled Molyneux was unrepentant, saying: "It's a sad day when someone has to be given a criminal record for defending the right to call himself an Englishman. It is political correctness gone mad. I'm very annoyed at the punishment."

<hr>

BATMAN CHRISTOPHER

London-born film director, writer and producer **Christopher Nolan** is best known for reviving the Batman movies, which had ceased in 1997 after the poor box office performance of the fourth instalment.

However, after co-writing the screenplay to his 2005 release *Batman Begins,* Nolan had a blockbuster on his hands. He was then director, producer and writer of *The Dark Knight* – released in 2008 – which smashed records in the U.S. by grossing over $158 million in its opening weekend.

EXECUTED CHRISTOPHER

Christopher Layer was executed at Tyburn, Middlesex (roughly where the Marble Arch now stands) on March 15th 1723, for the crime of high treason.

He had plotted to hire an assassin to murder the King of England but his plans were overheard in a public house and the news reached the relevant authorities who gained a warrant for his arrest.

At the time Layer had two women 'in keeping' and a search of their houses uncovered various letters that led to him being found guilty of treason and sentenced to death. He was taken to the Tower of London and confined there until he was hanged, drawn and quartered with his head being placed upon a spike for all to see!

The parents of **Christopher Johnson** were both convicted of fraud so it was perhaps no surprise that their son followed the same criminal path. He became a gambler and expert forger before sinking to the role of a common pickpocket, but he still lived in relative poverty.

After conspiring with John Stockdale, the duo robbed a wealthy landowner of £150 but this sum was quickly spent on 'wine, women and song' and the accomplices duly robbed many more people on the highways of Kent and Essex. A bungled attempt to rob an Edmonton postman led to Stockdale shooting the man dead and the fugitives soon being taken into custody – Stockdale later admitting his guilt to magistrates with Johnson unable to speak due to being intoxicated with drink!

The pair were quickly sentenced to death and hanged from a tree before their bodies were hung in chains on Winchmore Hill, Enfield.

Yorkshire-born **Christopher Wharton** was executed at York on March 28th 1600 for the crime of being a Roman Catholic priest. He was charged with high treason and was forced to hear Protestant sermons prior to his execution.

He refused both life and liberty in return for conformity and was beatified as a Catholic martyr in 1987.

IRISH CORNISHMAN CHRISTOPHER

Although more Cornish than a Cornish pasty,
Christopher Barry Morris represented the Republic of
Ireland at football on 34 occasions.

Born and brought up in the Cornish seaside town of
Newquay, Morris began his playing career with his local side
before signing for Sheffield Wednesday in 1982. It was after
moving to Glasgow Celtic in 1987 that his career flourished.

As his mother was born in County Mayo, he was drafted
into the Eire national side by new boss Jack Charlton – his
former manager at Wednesday. He played in both the
1988 European Championship Finals and the 1990 World
Cup Finals, playing all five games in the latter as Ireland
narrowly lost in the quarter-finals.

He won several honours in five years at Celtic and became
a crowd favourite at Middlesbrough before injury ended his
career in 1997. He has now returned to his roots, running
the family business, Morris Pasties.

⋙◆⋘

DAHMER CHRISTOPHER

Although jailed for life in 1992 for the slaying of social
worker Steve Lohman it was the murder of **Christopher
Scarver** (b. 1969), committed whilst inside the Columbia
Correctional Institution, in Portage, Wisconsin, that made
headlines across the world.

Those events took place in November 1994 when Scarver was placed on the same work detail as fellow convicted murderer Jesse Anderson and arguably the most gruesome serial killer of all time – Jeffrey Dahmer.

The infamous Dahmer killed seventeen men and boys – most of African or Asian descent – over a 13-year murderous spree that involved rape, torture, dismemberment, necrophilia and cannibalism and in 1992 was sentenced to fifteen life sentences, totalling 957 years.

On the morning of November 28th the prison guards left the three men unsupervised and Scarver duly attacked both Dahmer and Anderson with a heavy bar from the prison gymnasium – the former died on the way to hospital with the latter surviving for only two more days. After killing both men Scarver claimed that God told him to commit the crimes.

⸺≫•◆•≪⸺

CONCORDE CHRISTOPHER

Christopher John Dugmore Orlebar (b. 1945) was a pilot of the iconic Concorde supersonic plane, which was in service from January 1976 to November 2003. A product of French and British collaboration, the aircraft could fly from London to New York in under 3.5 hours (it takes traditional jet planes twice that time) and was seen as a flagship of the aviation industry, pioneering many technologies that are used in modern aircraft manufacture.

After qualifying as a civil aviation pilot, Orlebar joined BOAC (later renamed British Airways) in 1969 and became a VC10 pilot, instructor and navigator. He became a Concorde pilot in 1976 and remained in the cockpit for a decade before being appointed as a training captain on the Boeing 737.

He retired from British Airways in 2000 and is well known for his book *The Concorde Story*, which was first published in 1986 and remains the most comprehensive book written on the famous drooped nose plane, its sixth edition being published in 2004.

WHO CHRISTOPHER?

Christopher Dye is the co-ordinator of Tuberculosis (TB) Monitoring and Evaluation at the influential World Health Organisation (WHO). Graduating with a first-class degree in biology and a DPhil (Doctor of Philosophy) in zoology, Dye began working as an ecologist.

He was subsequently head of the Vector Biology and Epidemiology unit of the London School of Hygiene and Tropical Medicine, which has run major research projects in the likes of Kenya, Peru and Tanzania. The word 'vector' in epidemiology refers to an organism that does not cause a disease but conveys it from one host to another – examples being a mosquito that spreads malaria and yellow fever or a flea that carries the bubonic plague.

He joined WHO in 1996 to work on the epidemiology and control of tuberculosis, researching the disease that is still a major problem in many area of the world, despite TB being virtually under control in the developed world.

World Health Organisation figures state that two million people a year worldwide still die from the disease. In 2006, Dye was appointed the 37th Professor of Physics at the famous Gresham College, presenting public lectures like his predecessors have done in the City of London since 1597.

⋙◆⋘

BUM RAP CHRISTOPHER

When **Christopher Willever** broke into a Tobacco Hut store in Omaha, U.S. he struggled to squeeze through the security bars after having smashed the front window of the store. He did eventually squeeze through but as he did so his trousers ended up around his ankles.

However, probably not wanting to set off an alarm, he did not pull them back up so CCTV footage of the burglary showed the hilarious sight of Christopher crawling around on the floor of the shop with his trousers down.

When the footage was shown on local TV a member of the public tipped off the police after recognising the hapless thief – it is not known which end they actually identified!

Police duly raided his house and found several items belonging to the Tobacco Hut with the shop's owner pointing out the irony of the whole episode, as the store's slogan is 'best butts in town'.

———⟫◆⟪———

WHAT DID YOU SAY CHRISTOPHER?

An entire court case was conducted by mobile phone at Colchester Magistrates' Court in August 2008.

The defendant, **Christopher Coleman**, did not have a hearing aid and could not lip-read or understand sign language. He could however hear a mobile phone at high volume so the JPs and solicitors passed around another phone when they wanted to speak and Christopher kept his close to his ear.

He admitted harassing his former partner and calling her a 'fat cow' during thirty phone calls over two days. He was due to be sentenced when he had a hearing aid fitted!

———⟫◆⟪———

GOOD CHOICE CHRISTOPHER?

Despite his 1991 release Wicked Game becoming a worldwide hit it was the video to the song that made **Chris Isaak** the envy of most red-blooded males as he cavorted on a beach with a little known Danish fashion model, Helena Christensen.

The promo, shot completely in black and white, saw the brunette actually topless for most of the shoot, although this was disguised in the final cut. She played the role of Isaak's lover and her sexually charged performance catapulted her into the mainstream, becoming one of the 1990s' most prominent supermodels.

⟾⬧⟸

DON'T TRY THIS AT HOME CHRISTOPHER

In April 2008, a Newport coroner recorded a verdict of misadventure regarding the death of **Christopher Harris** who had been found by his partner after a sexual experiment had gone tragically wrong.

The divorced father of three was wearing a Russian biological warfare mask over his head and had run tubes from the hooded mask to a bottle of chloroform, which he intended to inhale. However, he inhaled far too much and died instantly from the fumes.

INSPIRATIONAL CHRISTOPHER

Motivational speaker **Chris Moon MBE** has inspired people around the world after being blown up in Mozambique – losing his lower right arm and leg – while working for a charity specialising in clearing landmines.

He is also one of the few Westerners to have survived kidnap in Cambodia by the feared Khmer Rouge. The former British Army officer has recovered from those setbacks to run some of the most demanding distance races in the world, climb mountains, cross countries on foot and generally inspire those around him.

———⊰•⊱———

MISSING CHRISTOPHER

When **Christopher MacNeil** left his family home in Romsey, Hampshire to join the Hare Krishna movement in 1979 his family worried that he would never return. He was only 17 years old when he joined the Hindu-based religion, popularised by the Beatles a decade earlier, but despite being missing for almost thirty years it was his sister, Caroline, who refused to believe he was dead.

She launched an attempt to find her elder brother, after being inspired by BBC television drama series *Missing*. The TV programme was based on the real life work of UK-based charity Missing People and it was to that organisation that Caroline turned to for help.

Eventually, after almost a year, the researchers tracked down Christopher to an Edinburgh address and he burst into tears when he read a letter from his sister who he had not seen since the day he left home. It transpired that Christopher had made attempts to contact his family but his efforts had not borne fruit and he had seemed set for a lonely future.

⇒◆◆◇⇐

FATHER CHRISTMAS CHRISTOPHER

The jolly Christmas visitor has a variety of names around the world including 'Kris Kringle', a derivative of the German 'das Christkind' which means 'Christ Child'.

⇒◆◆◇⇐

PARALYMPIC CHRISTOPHER

Among the 212 athletes who represented Britain at the 2008 Beijing Paralympics was Mansfield Harrier **Chris Martin** who had won discus gold eight years earlier in Sydney.

The Nottingham-born athlete had retired from competitive sport after competing in the Athens games of 2004 but after making a comeback in 2007 he realised he was still capable of world class performances.

He looked set to repeat his gold of 2000 but a last-gasp throw from Latvian Aigars Apinis of 20.47 metres set a new world record and agonisingly pushed Chris down into silver medal position.

CRICKETING CHRISTOPHER

When all-rounder **Chris Cowdrey** was appointed captain of the England cricket team in 1988 he followed in the footsteps of his father, Colin, who had captained his country on 27 occasions between 1959 and 1969.

They became only the second father and son combination to have captained England, equalling the record of Frank and George Mann who achieved the feat in the 1920s and 1940s, respectively.

At county level he played for Kent (1976-91) and Glamorgan (1992) and scored 12,252 first class runs at an average of 31.90, and grabbed 200 wickets at a 39.81 average.

After retiring he carved out a successful career as a commentator on the sport, working for radio station TalkSport and Sky Sports.

Christopher Chappell (b. 1955) is a right-handed batsman who played in Canada's first ever One-Day International, against Pakistan in the 1979 Cricket World Cup in England.

In total he played in six One-Day Internationals (ODIs) for his country of birth, his highest score being 35 against Sri Lanka.

Born in August 1886, **Christopher George Arthur Collier** was a batsman and slow bowler for Worcestershire. In total he appeared in 53 first-class games, scoring 1,021 runs at an average of 12.92, and took ten wickets at 36.9 runs per strike. He fought for his country in the Great War and was killed in action near Mametz, France just two days after his 30th birthday.

Chris Cairns was without doubt the finest all-rounder New Zealand has produced, claiming 3,320 runs (average: 33.53) and 218 wickets (average: 29.40) in 62 Test matches.

He is one of only seven men to have achieved the double of 200 wickets and 3,000 runs. He also appeared in 215 One-Day Internationals for his country – scoring 4,950 runs and taking 201 wickets – and in 2008 joined Chandigarh Lions in the booming Indian Cricket League.

Middlesbrough-born **Chris Old** played almost the whole of his first-class career with the county of his birth, Yorkshire.

Known by the nickname of Chilli, the right arm swing bowler also played in 46 Test matches for England, grabbing 143 wickets. After retiring he moved to the West Country and now runs a successful fish and chip shop in Praa Sands, Cornwall.

PUGH

Hurdles Christopher

Rotherham-born **Chris Rawlinson** (b. 1972) enjoyed great success as a 400 metres hurdles runner after having previously tried the pole vault, 100 metres hurdles and decathlon.

However, it was in the demanding one lap hurdles race that he became ranked British number one and in 2004 was placed in the world's top five by the IAAF (International Association of Athletics Federations).

He retired from the sport at the age of 33 in 2005 and in the following year married Australian double world 400m hurdles champion Jana Pittman, who he had coached since 1994. His medal haul included:

1997	World Student Games	4 x 400m relay	Bronze
1999	World Student Games	4 x 400m relay	Silver
2000	European Cup	400m hurdles	Gold
		4 x 400m	Silver
2002	World Cup	400m hurdles	Bronze
2002	Commonwealth Games	400m hurdles	Gold
		4 x 400m relay	Gold
2002	European Cup	400m hurdles	Bronze
2003	European Cup	400m hurdles	Gold
		4 x 400m relay	Silver
2004	European Cup	400m hurdles	Gold

Madonna Christopher

Brother of pop superstar Madonna, **Christopher G. Ciccone** (b. 1960) is an artist and interior decorator by profession and worked for his elder sibling throughout the 1980s and 1990s.

He first appeared next to Madonna in her 1982 video for Everybody and worked as her assistant, dresser, backup dancer, stylist and artistic director before the relationship between the pair started to deteriorate after Christopher co-wrote the book *Life with my sister Madonna*, released in July 2008.

The controversial publication lifted the lid on Madonna's personal life – painting his sister as a control freak, narcissist and cheapskate. It also criticised her lifestyle and her Kabbalah faith while 'Madge' has retorted by accusing her brother of being a habitual drug user… happy families…

⟹◆⟸

Ask the audience Christopher

Mainly known as the presenter of successful game show *Who Wants to be a Millionaire?*, **Christopher John Tarrant** (b. 1946) first came to public attention as a member of the anarchic Saturday morning kids' programme *Tiswas*.

Running from 1974 to 1982, the show totally ripped up the previous format of children's programmes and was a huge hit as a result, with both children and adults.

He is still regularly seen as the long-time host of *Tarrant on TV* while the acrimonious split from his wife, Ingrid, resulted in Tarrant reportedly paying around half of his estimated £25m fortune to his former spouse in 2006.

≫◆≪

CHRISTOPHER TRAGEDY

When the emergency services were called to a horrific house fire at a Shropshire mansion in the early hours on August 26th 2008 they discovered not only the grisly remains of three family members but also the bodies of the family's pet horses and dogs.

Further investigations suggested that millionaire **Christopher Foster** had killed both his wife and 15-year-old daughter (both having to be identified by dental records and DNA, respectively) before setting fire to the house, shooting the family pets and then taking his own life.

When the fire services arrived they found the front gate to the mansion had been blocked by a horse box and it later transpired that the businessman was suffering severe financial problems and it looked likely that his family would lose their £1.2m home.

The police also found CCTV footage from the property, showing a man believed to be Christopher Foster firing a rifle at a horsebox as his property burnt.

Sex and the City Christopher

Golden Globe-nominated actor **Christopher Noth** is best known in the UK for his role of Mr. Big in the highly successful U.S. programme *Sex and the City* (1998-2004).

After reprising his role as the Sarah Jessica Parker character's on-off love in the 2004 film of the same name he has played detective Mike Logan in *Law & Order: Criminal Intent*.

Before landing the part in the New York-based show the Wisconsin-born actor played a variety of roles in such popular cop shows as *Hill Street Blues* and *Homicide: Life on the Street*.

Astronaut Christopher

In 2001 **Chris Hadfield** (b. 1959) became the first Canadian to walk in space when he was part of a NASA mission to install a robotic arm to the International Space Station. In total he was outside for 14 hours and 54 minutes, travelling around the world ten times.

In 2006 the Canadian Royal Mint commemorated his achievement when they produced gold and silver coins. Growing up on a corn farm in southern Ontario, Hadfield had always been fascinated by flying and won a pilot scholarship at the age of just 16.

He duly joined the Armed Forces, training as a fighter pilot, and was then one of only four men chosen from 5,330 applicants to become a Canadian astronaut.

Born in Philadelphia, **Christopher J. Ferguson** qualified as an astronaut in 2000 after two years of training at the Johnson Space Center. His first mission came in September 2006 when he was part of a 12-day flight to restart assembly of the International Space Station.

In November 2008 he was part of the space shuttle crew that flew an astonishing 6 million miles on a 16-day mission. In his spare time, Chris drums for Max Q, a rock and roll band whose members all work at the Johnson Space Center in Houston, Texas.

Christopher J. Cassidy (b. 1970) completed his astronaut training at the relatively tender age of just 36 in February 2006, after having served ten years as a member of the crack U.S. Navy SEAL – Sea, Air and Land Forces – team.

In 2001 he was awarded a Bronze Star for leading a 9-day operation at the Zharwar Kili cave complex directly on the Afghan/Pakistan border and received a second Bronze Star in 2004 for combat leadership in Afghanistan.

There is every chance we have missed a Christopher, or two.

Let us know at **www.stripepublishing.co.uk**

ACKNOWLEDGEMENTS

Thanks firstly to my fiancée Michelle who supported me throughout as I hogged the PC in my little office in the search for weird and wonderful Christopher facts.

Also for her proofreading skills that ironed out a few blemishes! Also thanks to my soon-to-be stepdaughters, Kayleigh and Heather who suggested a few inclusions plus work colleagues Dave, Elaine and Margaret.

Many thanks also to British-born Sir Tim Berners-Lee who invented the World Wide Web in the late 1980s and made this publication possible.

Finally thanks to Dan Tester at Stripe Publishing for all his help and support throughout all the stages of the publication.

RECOMMENDED WEBSITES:

www.nasa.gov
www.wikipedia.org
www.paralympic.org
www.movies.about.com
www.usatoday.com
www.thesun.co.uk
www.crimelibrary.com
www.brainyhistory.com
www.bbc.co.uk
www.missingpeople.org.uk
www.olympic.org
www.business.timesonline.co.uk
www.guardian.co.uk
www.forbes.com
www.darwinawards.com
www.inventors.about.com
www.answers.com
www.coldplaying.com
www.luminarium.org
www.nfl.com
www.urbanmyths.com
www.babynamesbase.com
www.imbd.com
www.earth.google.com
www.meaning-of-names.com
www.itv.com/emmerdale
www.bbc.co.uk/eastenders
www.neighbours.com